THE
DALAI LAMA'S
CAT

THE DALAI LAMA'S CAT

DAVID MICHIE

HAY HOUSE

Australia • Canada • Hong Kong • India
South Africa • United Kingdom • United States

Hay House Publishers (India) Pvt. Ltd.
Muskaan Complex, Plot No.3, B-2 Vasant Kunj, New Delhi-110 070, India
Hay House Inc., PO Box 5100, Carlsbad, CA 92018-5100, USA
Hay House UK, Ltd., Astley House, 33 Notting Hill Gate, London W11 3JQ, UK
Hay House Australia Pty Ltd., 18/36 Ralph St., Alexandria NSW 2015, Australia
Hay House SA (Pty) Ltd., PO Box 990, Witkoppen 2068, South Africa
Hay House Publishing, Ltd., 17/F, One Hysan Ave., Causeway Bay, Hong Kong
Raincoast, 9050 Shaughnessy St., Vancouver, BC V6P 6E5, Canada
Email: contact@hayhouse.co.in
www.hayhouse.co.in

First Indian edition 2013
First reprint 2013
Second reprint 2014
Third reprint 2014
Fourth reprint 2015
Fifth reprint 2015
Sixth reprint 2015
Seventh reprint 2016
Eighth reprint 2017
Ninth reprint 2017
Tenth reprint 2017
Eleventh reprint 2017
Twelfth reprint 2018

ISBN 978-93-81431-71-9

FOR SALE IN THE INDIAN SUBCONTINENT ONLY

Printed at Repro Knowledgecast Limited, India

In loving memory of our own little Rinpoche,
Princess Wussik of the Sapphire Throne.

She brought us joy; we loved her well.

May this book be a direct cause for her,
and all living beings, to quickly and easily
attain complete enlightenment.

May all beings have happiness
and the true causes of happiness;

May all beings be free from suffering
and the true causes of suffering;

May all beings never be parted from the happiness that
is without suffering, the great joy of nirvana, liberation;

May all beings abide in peace and equanimity,
their minds free from attachment and aversion,
and free from indifference.

PROLOGUE

The idea came about one sunny Himalayan morning. There I was, lying in my usual spot on the first-floor windowsill—the perfect vantage point from which to maintain maximum surveillance with minimum effort—as His Holiness was bringing a private audience to a close.

I'm far too discreet to mention who the audience was with, except to say that she's a very famous Hollywood actress . . . you know, the *legally* blonde one, who does all the charity work for children and is quite well known for her love of donkeys. Yes, *her!*

It was as she was turning to leave the room that she glanced out the window, with its magnificent view of the snow-capped mountains, and noticed me for the first time.

"Oh! How adorable!" She stepped over to stroke my neck, which I acknowledged with a wide yawn and tremulous stretch of the front paws. "I didn't know you had a cat!" she exclaimed.

I am always surprised how many people make this observation—though not all are as bold as the American in giving voice to their astonishment. Why should His Holiness *not* have a cat—if, indeed, "having a cat" is a correct understanding of the relationship?

Besides, anyone with a particularly acute power of observation would recognize the feline presence in His Holiness's life by the stray hairs and occasional whisker I make it my business to leave on his person. Should you ever have the privilege of getting very close to the Dalai Lama and scrutinizing his robes, you will almost certainly discover a fine wisp of white fur, confirming that far from living alone, he shares his inner sanctum with a cat of impeccable—if undocumented—breeding.

It was exactly this discovery to which the queen of England's corgis reacted with such vigor when His Holiness visited Buckingham Palace—an incident of which the world media were strangely unaware.

But I digress.

Having stroked my neck, the American actress asked, "Does she have a name?"

"Oh, yes! Many names." His Holiness smiled enigmatically.

What the Dalai Lama said was true. Like many domestic cats, I have acquired a variety of names, some of them used frequently, others less so. One of them in particular is a name I don't much care for. Known among His Holiness's staff as my ordination name, it isn't a name the Dalai Lama himself has ever used—not the full version, at least. Nor is it a name I will disclose so long as I live. Not in this book, that's for sure.

Well . . . *definitely* not in this chapter.

"If only she could speak," continued the actress, "I'm sure she'd have such wisdom to share."

And so the seed was planted.

In the months that followed I watched His Holiness working on a new book: the many hours he spent making sure texts were correctly interpreted; the great time and care he took to ensure that every word he wrote conveyed the greatest possible meaning and benefit. More and more, I began to think that perhaps the time had come for me to write a book of my own—a book that would convey some of the wisdom I've learned sitting not at the feet of the Dalai Lama but even closer, on his lap. A book that would tell my own tale—not so much one of rags to riches as trash to temple. How I was rescued from a fate too grisly to contemplate, to become the constant companion of a man who is not only one of the world's greatest spiritual leaders and a Nobel Peace Prize Laureate but also a dab hand with a can opener.

Often in the late afternoon, after I feel His Holiness has already spent too many hours at his desk, I will hop off the windowsill, pad over to where he is working, and rub my furry body against his legs. If this doesn't get his attention, I sink my teeth politely but precisely into the tender flesh of his ankles. That always does it.

With a sigh, the Dalai Lama will push back his chair, scoop me up into his arms, and walk over to the window. As he looks into my big, blue eyes, the expression in his own is one of such immense love that it never ceases to fill me with happiness.

"My little 'bodhi*cat*va,'" he will sometimes call me, a play on *bodhisattva*, a Sanskrit term that in Buddhism refers to an enlightened being.

Together we gaze out at the panoramic vista that sweeps down the Kangra Valley. Through the open windows a gentle breeze carries fragrances of pine, Himalayan oak, and rhododendron, giving the air its pristine, almost magical, quality. In the warm embrace of the Dalai Lama, all distinctions dissolve completely—between observer and observed, between cat and lama, between the stillness of twilight and my deep-throated purr.

It is in these moments that I feel profoundly grateful to be the Dalai Lama's cat.

CHAPTER ONE

I have a defecating bull to thank for the event that was to change my very young life—and without which, dear reader, you would not be reading this book.

Picture a typical monsoonal afternoon in New Delhi. The Dalai Lama was on his way home from Indira Gandhi Airport, after a teaching trip to the United States. As his car made its way through the outskirts of the city, traffic was brought to a halt by a bull that had ambled into the center of the highway, where it proceeded to dump copiously.

Several cars back in the traffic jam, His Holiness was calmly gazing out the window, waiting for the traffic to start up again. As he sat there, his attention was drawn to a drama being played out at the side of the road.

Amid the clamor of pedestrians and bicyclists, food-stall proprietors and beggars, two ragged street children were anxious to bring their day's trading to an end. Earlier that morning, they had come across a litter of kittens, concealed behind a pile of burlap sacks in a back alley. Scrutinizing their discovery closely, they soon realized that they had fallen upon something of value. For the kittens were no garden-variety alley cats; they were clearly felines of a superior kind. The young boys were unfamiliar with the Himalayan breed, but in our sapphire eyes, handsome coloring, and lavish coat, they recognized a tradable commodity.

Snatching us from the cozy nest in which our mother had tended us, they thrust my siblings and me into the terrifying commotion of the street. Within moments my two elder sisters, who were much larger and more developed than the rest of us, had been exchanged for rupees—an event of such excitement that in the process I was dropped, landing painfully on the pavement and only narrowly avoiding being killed by a motor scooter.

The boys had much more trouble selling us two smaller, scrawnier kittens. For several hours they trudged the streets, shoving us vigorously at the windows of passing cars. I was much too young to be taken from our mother, and my tiny body was unable to cope. Failing fast for lack of milk and still in pain from my fall, I was barely conscious when the boys sparked the interest of an elderly passerby, who had been thinking about a kitten for his granddaughter.

Gesturing to set us two remaining kittens on the ground, he squatted on his haunches and inspected us closely. My older brother padded across the corrugated dirt at the side of the road, mewing imploringly for milk. When I was prodded from behind to induce some movement, I managed only a single, lurching step forward before collapsing in a mud puddle.

It was exactly this scene that His Holiness witnessed.

And the one that followed.

A sale price agreed on, my brother was handed over to the toothless old man. I, meantime, was left mired in filth while the two boys debated what to do with me, one of them shoving me roughly with his big toe. They decided I was unsaleable, and grabbing a week-old sports page of the *Times of India* that had blown into a nearby gutter, they wrapped me like a piece of rotten meat destined for the nearest rubbish heap.

I began to suffocate inside the newspaper. Every breath became a struggle. Already weak from fatigue and starvation, I felt the flame of life inside me flicker dangerously low. Death seemed inevitable in those final, desperate moments.

Except that His Holiness dispatched his attendant first. Fresh off the plane from America, the Dalai Lama's attendant happened to have two $1 bills tucked in his robes. He handed these to the boys, who scampered away, speculating with great excitement about how much the dollars would fetch when converted into rupees.

Unwrapped from the death trap of the sports page ("Bangalore Crushes Rajasthan by 9 Wickets" read the headline), I was soon resting comfortably in the back of the Dalai Lama's car. Moments later, milk had been bought from a street vendor and was being dripped into my mouth as His Holiness willed life back into my limp form.

I remember none of the details of my rescue, but the story has been recounted so many times that I know it by heart. What I do remember is waking up in a sanctuary of such infinite warmth that for the first time since being wrenched from our burlap nest that morning, I felt that all was well. Looking about to discover the source of my newfound nourishment and safety, I found myself looking directly into the Dalai Lama's eyes.

How do I describe the first moment of being in the presence of His Holiness?

It is as much a feeling as a thought—a deeply heartwarming and profound understanding that all is well. As I came to realize later, it is as though for the first time you become aware that your own true nature is one of boundless love and compassion. It has been there all along, but the Dalai Lama sees it and reflects it back to you. He perceives your Buddha nature, and this extraordinary revelation often moves people to tears.

In my own case, swaddled in a piece of marooncolored fleece on a chair in His Holiness's office, I was also aware of another fact—one of the greatest importance to all cats: I was in the home of a cat lover.

As strongly as I sensed this, I was also aware of a less sympathetic presence across the coffee table. Back in Dharamsala, His Holiness had resumed his schedule of audiences and was fulfilling a long-standing commitment to be interviewed by a visiting history professor from Britain. I couldn't possibly tell you who exactly, just that he came from one of England's two most famous Ivy League universities.

The professor was penning a tome on Indo-Tibetan history and seemed irked to find he was not the exclusive focus of the Dalai Lama's attention.

"A stray?" he exclaimed, after His Holiness briefly explained the reason why I was occupying the seat between them.

"Yes," confirmed the Dalai Lama, before responding not so much to what the visitor had said as to the tone of voice in which he had said it. Regarding the history professor with a kindly smile, he spoke in that rich, warm baritone with which I was to become so familiar.

"You know, Professor, this stray kitten and you have one very important thing in common."

"I can't imagine," responded the professor coolly.

"Your life is the most important thing in the world to you," said His Holiness. "Same for this kitten."

From the pause that followed, it was evident that for all his erudition, the professor had never before been presented with such a startling idea.

"Surely you're not saying that the life of a human and the life of an animal are of the same value?" he ventured.

"As humans we have much greater potential, of course," His Holiness replied. "But the way we all want very much to stay alive, the way we cling to our particular experience of consciousness—in *this* way human and animal are equal."

"Well, perhaps some of the more complex mammals . . . " The professor was battling against this troubling thought. "But not all animals. I mean, for instance, not *cockroaches*."

"Including cockroaches," said His Holiness, undeterred. "Any being that has consciousness."

"But cockroaches carry filth and disease. We *have* to spray them."

His Holiness rose and walked over to his desk, where he picked up a large matchbox. "Our cockroach carrier," he said. "Much better than spraying. I am sure," he continued, delivering his trademark chuckle. "*You* don't want to be chased by a giant spraying toxic gas."

The professor acknowledged this bit of self-evident but uncommon wisdom in silence.

"For all of us with consciousness"—the Dalai Lama returned to his seat—"our life is very precious. Therefore, we need to protect all sentient beings very much. Also, we must recognize that we share the same two basic wishes: the wish to enjoy happiness and the wish to avoid suffering."

These are themes I have heard the Dalai Lama repeat often and in limitless ways. Yet every time he speaks with such vivid clarity and impact, it is as though he is expressing them for the first time.

"We all share these wishes. But also the way we look for happiness and try to avoid discomfort is the same. Who among us does not enjoy a delicious meal? Who does not wish to sleep in a safe, comfortable bed? Author, monk—or stray kitten—we are all equal in that."

Across the coffee table, the history professor shifted in his seat.

"Most of all," the Dalai Lama said, leaning over and stroking me with his index finger, "all of us just want to be loved."

By the time the professor left later that afternoon, he had a lot more to think about than his tape recording of the Dalai Lama's views on Indo-Tibetan history. His Holiness's message was challenging. Confronting, even. But it wasn't one that could easily be dismissed . . . as we were to discover.

In the days that followed, I quickly became familiar with my new surroundings. The cozy nest His Holiness created for me out of an old fleece robe. The changing light in his rooms as the sun rose, passed over us, and set each day, and the tenderness with which he and his two executive assistants fed me warm milk until I was strong enough to begin eating solid food.

I also began exploring, first the Dalai Lama's own suite, then out beyond it, to the office shared by the two executive assistants. The one seated closest to the door, the young, roly-poly monk with the smiling face and soft hands, was Chogyal. He helped His Holiness with monastic matters. The older, taller one, who sat opposite him, was Tenzin. Always in a dapper suit, with hands that had the clean tang of carbolic soap, he was a professional diplomat and cultural attaché who assisted the Dalai Lama in secular matters.

That first day I wobbled around the corner into their office, there was an abrupt halt in the conversation.

"Who is this?" Tenzin wanted to know.

Chogyal chuckled as he lifted me up and put me on his desk, where my eye was immediately caught by the bright blue top of a Bic pen. "The Dalai Lama rescued her while driving out of Delhi," Chogyal said, repeating the attendant's story as I flicked the Bic top across his desk.

"Why does she walk so strangely?" the other wanted to know.

"Apparently she was dropped on her back."

"Hmm." Tenzin sounded doubtful as he leaned forward, scrutinizing me closely. "Perhaps she was malnourished, being the smallest kitten. Does she have a name?"

"No," Chogyal said. Then, after he and I had batted the plastic pen top back and forth across his desk a few times, he exclaimed, "We'll have to give her one!" He seemed enthusiastic about the challenge. "An ordination name. What do you think—Tibetan or English?" (In Buddhism, when someone becomes a monk or nun they are given an ordination name to mark their new identity.)

Chogyal suggested several possibilities before Tenzin said, "It's better not to force these things. I'm sure something will present itself as we get to know her better."

As usual, Tenzin's advice was both wise and prophetic— unfortunately for me, as things turned out. Chasing the pen top, I progressed from Chogyal's desk halfway across Tenzin's, before the older man seized my small, fluffy form and put me down on the rug.

"You'd better stay there," he said. "I have a letter here from His Holiness to the Pope, and we don't want paw prints all over it."

Chogyal laughed. "Signed on his behalf by His Holiness's Cat."

"HHC," Tenzin shot back. In official correspondence, His Holiness is frequently referred to as HHDL. "That can be her provisional title until we find a suitable name."

Beyond the executive assistants' office was a corridor that led past more offices, toward a door that was kept carefully closed. I knew from talk in the executive assistants' office that the door led to many places, including Downstairs, Outside, The Temple, and even Overseas. This was the door through which all His Holiness's visitors came and went. It opened onto a whole new world. But in those early days, as a very small kitten, I was perfectly content to remain on this side of it.

Having spent my first days on Earth in a back alley, I had little understanding of human life—and no idea how unusual my new circumstances were. When His Holiness got out of bed every morning at 3 A.M. to meditate for five hours, I would follow him and curl up in a tight knot beside him, basking in his warmth and energy. I thought that most people started each day in meditation.

When visitors came to see His Holiness, I saw that they always presented him with a white scarf, or *kata*, which he then returned to them with a blessing. I assumed this was how humans usually greeted visitors. I was also aware that many people who visited His Holiness had traveled very long distances to do so; that, too, seemed perfectly normal to me.

Then one day Chogyal picked me up in his arms and tickled my neck. "Are you wondering who all these people are?" he asked, following my gaze to the many framed photographs on the wall of the executive assistants' office. Gesturing to a few of the photos, he said, "These are the past eight presidents of the United States, meeting His Holiness. He is a very special person, you know."

I did know, because he always made sure my milk was warm—but not too hot—before giving it to me.

"He is one of the world's greatest spiritual leaders," Chogyal continued. "We believe he is a living Buddha. You must have a very close karmic connection to him. It would be most interesting to know what that is."

A few days later, I found my way down the corridor to the small kitchen and sitting area where some of the Dalai Lama's staff went to relax, have their lunch, or make tea. Several monks were sitting on a sofa, watching a recorded news item on His Holiness's recent visit to the U.S. By now they all knew who I was—in fact, I had become the office mascot. Hopping up on the lap of one of the monks, I allowed him to stroke me as I watched TV.

Initially, all I could see was a huge crowd of people with a tiny red dot in the center, while His Holiness's voice could be heard quite clearly. But as the news clip progressed, I realized that the red dot was His Holiness, in the center of a vast indoor sports arena. It was a scene that was replayed in every city he visited, from New York to San Francisco. The newscaster commented that the huge crowds of people who came out to see him in every city showed that he was more popular than many rock stars.

Little by little, I began to realize just how extraordinary the Dalai Lama was, and how highly regarded. And perhaps because of Chogyal's comment about our "very close karmic connection," at some stage I started to believe that I must be rather special, too. After all, I was the one His Holiness had rescued from the gutters of New Delhi. Had he recognized in me a kindred spirit—a sentient being on the same spiritual wavelength as he?

When I heard His Holiness tell visitors about the importance of loving kindness, I would purr contentedly, certain in the knowledge that this was exactly what I thought, too. When he opened my evening can of Snappy Tom, it seemed as obvious to me as it was to him that all sentient beings wanted to fulfill the same basic needs. And as he stroked my bulging tummy after my dinner, it seemed equally clear that he was right; each of us does just want to be loved.

There had been some talk around this time about what would happen when His Holiness left on a three-week trip to Australia and New Zealand. With this and many other travels planned, should I remain in the Dalai Lama's quarters, or would it be better if I were found a new home?

New home? The very idea of it was crazy! I was HHC and had quickly become a vital part of the establishment. There was no one I'd rather live with than the Dalai Lama. And I'd come to treasure other parts of my daily routine, whether it was sunning myself on the windowsill as His Holiness talked to visitors, or eating the delicious food he and his staff served me on a saucer, or listening to lunchtime concerts with Tenzin.

Although His Holiness's cultural attaché was Tibetan, he was a graduate of Oxford University in England, where he had studied in his early 20s, developing a taste for all things European. Every day at lunchtime, unless there was very pressing business to attend to, Tenzin would get up from his desk, take out the small, plastic box of lunch his wife had prepared for him, and make his way along the corridor to the first-aid room. Seldom used for that purpose, it contained a single bed, a medicine cabinet, an armchair, and a portable sound system that belonged to Tenzin. Following him into the room out of curiosity one day, I watched him settle back in the armchair and press a button on the remote control of the sound system. Suddenly, the room was filled with music. Eyes closed, he rested his head against the back of the chair, a smile appearing on his lips.

"Bach's *Prelude in C Major*, HHC," he told me after the short piano piece ended. I hadn't realized he even knew that I was in the room with him. "Isn't it exquisite? One of my all-time favorites. So simple—just a single melody line, no harmony, but conveying such depth of emotion!"

It turned out to be the first in an almost daily series of lessons in music and Western culture that I received from Tenzin. He seemed to genuinely welcome my presence as a being with whom he could share his enthusiasm for this operatic aria or that string quartet—or sometimes, for variety, the reenactment of some historical event in a radio drama.

While he ate whatever was in his plastic lunch box, I would curl up on the first-aid bed—a liberty he indulged since it was just the two of us. My appreciation of music and Western culture began to develop, one lunch hour at a time.

Then one day, something unexpected happened. His Holiness was over at the temple, and The Door was left open. By then I had grown into an adventurous kitten, no longer content to spend all her time cosseted in fleece. Prowling along the corridor in search of excitement when I saw The Door ajar, I knew I had to go through it, to explore the many places that lay beyond.

Downstairs. Outside. Overseas.

Somehow I made my shaky way down two flights of stairs, grateful for the carpeting, as my descent accelerated out of control and I landed in an undignified bundle at the bottom. Picking myself up, I continued across a short hallway and went Outside.

It was the first time I'd been outdoors since being plucked from the gutters of New Delhi. There was a bustle, a feeling of energy, with people walking in every direction. I hadn't gotten very far before I heard a chorus of high-pitched squeals and the pounding of many feet on the pavement. A tour group of Japanese schoolgirls caught sight of me and took pursuit.

I panicked. Racing as fast as my unsteady hind legs would take me, I lurched away from the shrieking horde. I could hear them gaining ground. There was no way I could outrun them. The leather of their shoes slapping the pavement became a thunder!

Then I spotted a small gap between brick columns that supported a verandah floor. An opening that led under the building. It was a tight squeeze, and I had very little time. Plus, I had no idea where the gap led. But as I bolted inside, the pandemonium abruptly ended. I found myself in a large crawl space between the ground and wooden floorboards. It was dark and dusty, and there was a constant, dull drumming of foot traffic overhead. But at least I was safe. I wondered how long I would need to stay there until the schoolgirls had gone away. Brushing a cobweb from my face, I decided not to risk another attack.

As my eyes and ears adjusted to my surroundings, I became aware of a scratching noise—a sporadic but insistent gnawing. I paused, nostrils flared, as I searched the air. For along with the sound of incisors chomping came a pungent whiff that set my whiskers tingling. My reaction, instantaneous and powerful, triggered a reflex I hadn't even known I possessed.

Even though I had never before seen a mouse, I recognized it immediately as a creature of prey. It was clinging to brickwork, its head half-buried in a wooden beam that it was hollowing out with its large front teeth.

I moved stealthily, my approach masked by the constant sound of footfalls on the floor above.

Instinct took over. With a single swipe of my front paw, I swept the rodent off balance and onto the ground, where it lay stunned. Leaning down, I sank my teeth into its neck. Its body went limp.

I knew exactly what I must do next. Prey secured in my mouth, I padded back to the gap between the brick columns, checked the pavement traffic outside, and, seeing no Japanese schoolchildren, hurried back along the pavement and back inside the building. Dashing across the hallway, I made my way up the stairs to The Door. Shut tight.

Now what? I sat there for quite some time, wondering how long I would have to wait, until finally someone from His Holiness's staff arrived. Recognizing me but paying no attention to the trophy in my mouth, he let me in. I padded down the corridor and around the corner.

Because the Dalai Lama was still at the temple, I went to the office of the executive assistants, dropping the mouse and announcing my arrival with an urgent meow. Responding to the unfamiliar tone, Chogyal and Tenzin both turned and looked at me in surprise as I stood there proudly, with the mouse on the carpet at my feet.

Their reaction was nothing like I had expected. Exchanging a sharp glance, they both shot out of their chairs. Chogyal picked me up, and Tenzin knelt down over the motionless mouse.

"Still breathing," he said. "Probably in shock."

"The printer box," Chogyal said, directing him to the empty cardboard box from which he had just removed a fresh ink cartridge.

Using an old envelope as a brush, Tenzin herded the mouse into the empty container. He regarded it closely. "Where do you think—?"

"This one has cobwebs on its whiskers," observed Chogyal, cocking his head in my direction.

This one? It?! Was that any way to refer to HHC?

At that moment, the Dalai Lama's driver came into the office. Tenzin handed him the box with instructions that the mouse was to be observed and, if it recovered, to be released in the forest nearby.

"HHC must have gotten out," said the driver, meeting my blue-eyed gaze.

Chogyal was still holding me, not in his usual affectionate embrace but as though restraining a savage beast. "HHC. I'm not sure about that title anymore," he said.

"It was only a provisional title," concurred Tenzin, returning to his desk. "But His Holiness's Mouser doesn't seem appropriate."

Chogyal put me back on the carpet.

"What about just 'Mouser' for an ordination name?" suggested the driver. But because of his strong, Tibetan accent, it sounded like "Mousie."

All three men were now looking at me intently. The conversation had taken a dangerous turn that I have regretted ever since.

"You can't have just 'Mousie,'" said Chogyal. "It has to be Something Mousie or Mousie Something."

"Mousie Monster?" contributed Tenzin.

"Mousie Slayer?" suggested Chogyal.

There was a pause before the driver came out with it. "What about Mousie-Tung?" he suggested.

All three men burst out laughing as they looked down at my small, fluffy form.

Tenzin turned mock-serious as he regarded me directly. "Compassion is all very well. But do you think His Holiness should be sharing his quarters with Mousie-Tung?"

"Or leaving Mousie-Tung in charge for three weeks when he visits Australia?" mused Chogyal, as the three collapsed in laughter again.

Getting up, I stalked from the room, ears pressed back firmly and tail slashing.

In the hours that followed, as I sat in the tranquil sunlight of His Holiness's window, I began to realize the enormity of what I'd done. For almost all my young life I had been listening to the Dalai Lama point out that the lives of all sentient beings are as important to them as our own life is to us. But how much attention had I paid to that on the one and only occasion I was out in the world?

As for the truth that all beings wish to be happy and to avoid suffering—that thought hadn't crossed my mind while I was stalking the mouse. I had simply let instinct take over. Not for one moment had I considered my actions from the *mouse's* point of view.

I was beginning to realize that just because an idea is simple, it isn't necessarily easy to follow. Purring in agreement with high-sounding principles meant nothing unless I actually *lived* by them.

I wondered if His Holiness would be told my new "ordination name"—the grim reminder of the greatest folly of my young life. Would he be so horrified when he heard what I'd done that he would banish me from this beautiful haven forever?

Fortunately for me, the mouse recovered. And when His Holiness returned, he was immediately caught up in a series of meetings.

It wasn't until late in the evening that he mentioned the subject. He had been sitting up in bed reading before closing his book, removing his glasses, and placing them on the bedside table.

"They told me what happened," he murmured, reaching over to where I was dozing nearby. "Sometimes our instinct, our negative conditioning, can be overpowering. Later we regret very much what we have done. But that is no reason to give up on yourself—the buddhas, they have not given up on you. Instead, learn from your mistake and move on. Like that."

He turned out the bedside light, and as we both lay there in the darkness, I purred gently in appreciation.

"Tomorrow we start again," he said.

The next day, His Holiness was going through the few pieces of mail his executive assistants had selected for his attention from the sackfuls that arrived every morning.

Holding up a letter and a book sent by the history professor from England, he turned to Chogyal. "This is very nice."

"Yes, Your Holiness," Chogyal agreed, studying the glossy cover of the book.

"I am not thinking about the book," said His Holiness, "but the letter."

"Oh?"

"After reflecting on our conversation, the professor says he has stopped using snail bait on his roses. Instead, he now releases the snails over the garden wall."

"Very good!" said Chogyal with a smile.

The Dalai Lama looked directly at me. "We liked meeting him, didn't we?" I remembered that at the time, I had thought how deeply unenlightened the professor seemed. But after what I'd done yesterday, I was hardly one to judge.

"It shows that we all have the ability to change, doesn't it, Mousie?"

CHAPTER TWO

Even though cats spend most of the day dozing comfortably, we like our humans to keep busy. Not in a noisy or intrusive way—just active enough to entertain us during those periods when we choose to remain awake. Why else do you think most cats have a favorite theater seat—a preferred spot on a windowsill, porch, gatepost, or cupboard top? Don't you realize, dear reader, that you are our entertainment?

One of the reasons why it's so congenial living at Jokhang, as the Dalai Lama's temple complex is known, is for exactly this reason: there is always something going on.

Before 5 A.M. each morning, the temple complex comes alive with the sound of sandaled feet on the pavement as the monks from Namgyal Monastery converge for their morning meditations. By this time, His Holiness and I have been meditating for two hours, but as

I become aware of the stirring outside, I like to get up, stretch my front legs luxuriantly in front of me, and perhaps take a few limbering-up scratches of the carpet, before heading over to my usual position on the windowsill. From there I watch the reassuring circadian performance begin to be reenacted, for in monastic life, almost every day is the same.

It begins with golden squares flickering to life across the horizon, as lamps are lit in the temple and the monks' quarters. In the summer, the early morning breeze carries clouds of purple incense—along with dawn chants—through the open window, just as the sky begins to light up in the east.

By the time the monks emerge from the temple at nine in the morning, His Holiness and I have both eaten breakfast, and he is already at his desk. Morning briefings with his advisers follow, and down in the temple, the monks return for a well-ordered daily routine that includes reciting texts, attending teachings, debating points of philosophy in the courtyard, and meditating. These activities are interrupted only by two meals and come to an end around 10 o'clock at night.

After that, the younger monks are expected to return home and memorize texts until midnight. More is demanded of the older ones, who frequently study and debate until one or two in the morning. The period in the middle of the night when there is no activity at all lasts only a few hours.

Center stage in His Holiness's suite, meantime, there is a constant procession of visitors: world-famous politicians, celebrities, and philanthropists, as well as those who are less well known but sometimes more intriguing, such as the Nechung Oracle, whom His Holiness sometimes consults. A medium between the material world and spiritual realms, the Nechung Oracle is the State Oracle of Tibet. He warned of difficulties with China as early as 1947 and continues to help with important decisions, going into an induced trance state, sometimes as part of an elaborate ceremony during which he offers prophecies and advice.

You would think that finding myself in such a stimulating and comfortable environment would make me the happiest cat that ever played the cello, as we cats refer to that most delicate part of our grooming regimen when we attend to our nether regions. But alas, dear reader, in those early months living with the Dalai Lama, you would be wrong.

Perhaps it was because I had, until so recently, only ever known what it was like to be one of a litter of four. Maybe it was an absence of contact with any other sentient being blessed with fur and whiskers. Whatever the reason, I not only felt very alone but also came to believe that my happiness would be complete only with the presence of another cat.

The Dalai Lama knew this. Taking care of me from that first moment in the car with the utmost tenderness and compassion, he nurtured me through those early weeks, constantly attentive to my well-being.

Which was why, one day soon after the mouse incident, when I was loitering in the passage, feeling lost and uncertain of what to do, he caught sight of me on his way to the temple and turning to Chogyal, who was accompanying him, said, "Perhaps little Snow Lion would like to come with us?"

Snow Lion?! I loved the name. As he picked me up in his robed arms, I purred with approval. Snow lions are celestial animals in Tibet, representing unconditional happiness. They are animals of great beauty, vibrancy, and delight.

"We have a big day ahead," His Holiness told me as we went downstairs. "First a visit to the temple to watch the examinations. Then Mrs. Trinci is coming to prepare lunch for today's visitor. And you like Mrs. Trinci, don't you?"

Like was hardly the word. I *adored* Mrs. Trinci, or to be more specific, Mrs. Trinci's diced chicken liver—a dish she made especially for my delectation.

Whenever catering was required for a special occasion or visiting dignitary, Mrs. Trinci was called in. More than 20 years earlier, someone in the Dalai Lama's office, while planning a banquet for a high-powered delegation from the Vatican, had discovered the Italian widow living locally. Mrs. Trinci's culinary flair had quite effortlessly transcended all previous catering, and she was soon installed as the Dalai Lama's favorite chef.

An elegant woman in her 50s, with a penchant for flamboyant dresses and extravagant costume jewelry, she would sweep into Jokhang on a wave of nervous excitement. Assuming instant control of the kitchen from the moment she arrived, she pulled everyone present, not just the kitchen hands, into her vortex. On one of her earliest visits, she had ordered the abbot of Gyume Tantric College, who happened to be walking past, into the kitchen, where she immediately tied an apron around his neck and set him to dicing carrots.

Mrs. Trinci knew no protocol and brooked no dissent. Spiritual advancement was of little relevance with a banquet for eight to prepare. Her operatic temperament was the very opposite of the calm humility of most of the monks, but there was something about her vivacity, her intensity, her passion that they found utterly beguiling.

And they loved her generous heart. She always made sure that along with His Holiness's meal, an appetizing stew was left on the stove for his staff, and apple strudel, chocolate gateau, or some other heavenly confection was left in the fridge.

The first time she saw me, she declared me to be The Most Beautiful Creature That Ever Lived, and from that day on, no visit to the Dalai Lama's kitchen was complete without her producing, from one of her many grocery bags, some succulent morsels brought especially for me. Placing me on a countertop, she would watch me closely, her amber, mascara-lashed eyes swooning as I noisily devoured a saucer of chicken pot-au-feu, turkey casserole, or filet mignon. I was contemplating exactly this prospect as Chogyal carried me across the courtyard toward the temple.

I had never been inside the temple before and could think of no better way to make my first entrance than in His Holiness's entourage. The temple is an amazing, light-filled building with very high ceilings, vivid wallhangings of deities in richly embroidered silks, and multicolored victory banners cascading down the walls. There are large Buddha statues with rows of gleaming brass bowls set out before them, along with symbolic offerings of food, incense, flowers, and perfume. Hundreds of monks were seated on cushions, waiting for the exams to begin, and the low buzz of their chatter continued even after the Dalai Lama arrived. Usually he would make a formal entrance at the front of the temple, taking his place on the teaching throne amid an awed hush. But today he slipped in the back, not wanting to draw attention to himself or distract the monks who were about to be examined.

Every year, novice monks compete for a limited number of places to study for the Geshe degree. The highest qualification in Tibetan Buddhism, in some ways like a doctorate, the Geshe degree takes 12 years to complete. It demands flawless recall of core texts and an ability to analyze and debate subtle philosophical differences, not to mention many hours of meditation practice. For most of the 12 years of the course, geshe trainees work 20 hours every day, following a rigorous schedule of study. But despite the very great demands placed on them, there are always more novice monks seeking entrance than there are places available.

At today's exam, four novice monks were being tested. In accordance with tradition, they began by answering the examiners' questions in front of the assembled Namgyal community, an arrangement that was daunting but also open and transparent. Watching the proceedings was good preparation for the younger novice monks, who would one day also have to stand before their peers.

In the back row of the temple, sitting next to the Dalai Lama on Chogyal's lap, I listened as two Bhutanese brothers, a Tibetan boy, and a French student all had the chance to impress their audience by answering questions about subjects like karma and the nature of reality. The Bhutanese brothers gave correct, rote answers and the Tibetan boy also quoted directly from the assigned text, but the French student went further, demonstrating that he had not only learned the concepts but also understood them. Throughout all of this, the Dalai Lama smiled warmly.

Next, in debate with several senior monks who tried to catch the students with clever arguments, the same pattern was followed. The Bhutanese and Tibetan students stuck carefully to textbook answers, while the French boy launched provocative counterarguments of his own, prompting quite some amusement in the temple.

Finally it was time to recite texts, and again the Himalayan students were flawless in their recall. Asked to recite the *Heart Sutra*, a short text that is one of Buddha's most famous teachings, the French student began in a clear, strong voice. But for some reason, midway through he faltered. There was a long, puzzled silence—and, it seemed, some whispered prompting—before he began again, somewhat less confidently, only to lapse completely. He turned to his examiners with an apologetic shrug. They gestured for him to return to his seat.

A short time later the examiners announced their verdict: the Bhutanese and Tibetan novices were accepted for Geshe studies. Only the French boy was unsuccessful.

I could feel the Dalai Lama's sadness as the announcement was made. The examiners' decision was inevitable, but even so . . .

"There is less emphasis on rote learning in the West," Chogyal murmured to His Holiness, who nodded in agreement. Asking Chogyal to take care of me, His Holiness had the disappointed-looking French novice taken to a private room at the back of the temple, where he revealed to the young man that he had been present throughout the examination.

Who can say what words passed between the two of them that day? But after a few minutes, the French boy returned, looking both consoled and overwhelmed to have been the subject of the Dalai Lama's attention. I was coming to learn that His Holiness has a very particular ability to help guide individuals to their highest personal purpose—one that would bring great happiness and benefit to both themselves and many others.

"Sometimes I hear people speaking despondently about the future of Buddhism," His Holiness said to Chogyal, as we returned to his quarters later. "I wish they could come to the examinations to experience what we saw here today. There are so many novices, so committed and of such a high caliber. My only wish is that we had places for them all."

By the time we had returned from the temple, Mrs. Trinci was in full command of the kitchen, to which I made my way directly. His Holiness had distracted me from my loneliness with the visit to the temple that morning. Now Mrs. Trinci continued the entertainment. She was wearing an emerald green dress with dangling gold earrings and matching bracelets that clanked together every time she moved her arms. Her long, dark hair on this visit seemed to have a reddish tinge.

Mrs. Trinci's life rarely followed the same smooth regularity as that of the permanent residents of Jokhang, and today was no exception. The present crisis had been provoked by a 2 A.M. power cut. Mrs. Trinci had gone to bed believing she would wake to a crisp meringue base in her oven, which she had set to the prescribed low, overnight temperature. Instead she had woken to a soggy mess beyond redemption—with only seven hours before His Holiness's VIP guest arrived.

There had followed the frantic whipping up of a new base, a high-risk ramping up of the oven temperature, and an elaborate plan to have the base couriered to Jokhang at 1 P.M.—long after she had arrived to prepare the main course but before dessert was to be served.

"Would it not be easier to prepare another dessert?" Tenzin had suggested, dangerously, on learning of the drama. "Something simple like—"

"It *has* to be a Pavlova. She's Australian!" Mrs. Trinci flung a stainless steel spatula into the sink with a crash. She always incorporated an element of a guest's national cuisine, and today was to be no exception. "What's Australian about Melanzane Parmigiana?"

Tenzin took a step back.

"Or vegetable ragout?!"

"I was just suggesting—"

"Well, don't suggest! *Zitto!* Hush! No time for suggestions!"

His Holiness's executive assistant made a tactical retreat.

Despite all the histrionics, Mrs. Trinci's meal was, as always, a gastronomic triumph. The Pavlova betrayed no hint of the crisis from which it had been brought forth; it was a perfect meringue base crowned by equally perfect individual meringues, filled with a cornucopia of glistening fruit and whipped cream.

And Mrs. Trinci had not forgotten The Most Beautiful Creature That Ever Lived. She treated me to a helping of leftover beef casserole so generous that I had to meow to be put down from the kitchen counter after eating, being too stuffed to jump down on my own.

Having bestowed several appreciative licks on Mrs. Trinci's bejeweled fingers, I waddled through to the reception room in which the Dalai Lama and his visitor were now sipping tea. Our lunchtime visitor that day was the Venerable Robina Courtin, a nun who had devoted much time to helping prisoners rehabilitate their lives through her Liberation Prison Project. The subject of prison conditions in America was being discussed as I made my entrance and headed over to a favorite woolen rug to perform the customary post-prandial face-washing.

"Conditions vary greatly," the nun was saying. "Some facilities lock up their prisoners for most of the day in cells that feel like basement cages with no natural light. We have to sit on one side of a small hole in an iron door to talk to a prisoner on the other side. In such circumstances, there seems little hope of rehabilitation.

"But there are many other facilities," she continued, "where the focus is more positive—on training and motivating people to change. There's no escaping the institutional atmosphere, but cell doors are open for more of the day, and there are sports and recreational activities, as well as TV, computer access, and libraries."

She paused, smiling as she remembered something. "There was this group of lifers I got to know quite well when teaching meditation classes in Florida. One of them asked me, 'What happens in a nunnery, day to day?'"

She shrugged. "So I told him that we get up at five in the morning for the first meditation session. Well, that was much too early for him! Roll call in the jail is a leisurely 7 A.M. I explained that our day is structured from the time we get up until we retire at 10 P.M., with a strong emphasis on learning and studying, and working in the nunnery gardens to grow the fruit and vegetables we eat." She grimaced. "He didn't like the sound of that either."

The others were smiling.

"I said that we didn't have a TV or newspapers or alcohol or computers. Unlike the prisoners in a jail, the nuns can't earn money to buy special treats. And there are certainly no conjugal visits!"

The Dalai Lama chuckled.

"That's when he came out with the most extraordinary thing," she went on. "Without even realizing what he was saying, he suggested, 'If it all gets too hard, you could always come and live with us here.'"

Everyone in the room burst out laughing.

"He actually felt sorry for me!" Robina's eyes sparkled. "It seemed to him that conditions were even harsher in the nunnery than in jail."

His Holiness leaned forward in his chair, stroking his chin thoughtfully. "Isn't that interesting? Only this morning at the temple, we saw novice monks competing for admission to the monastery. There are too many novices and not enough places. But turning to the jail, nobody wants to go there, even though the conditions are easier than in a monastery. This proves that it is not so much the circumstances of our lives that make us happy or unhappy but the way we see them."

There were murmurs of agreement.

"Do we believe that, whatever our circumstances, we have the chance to live happy and meaningful lives?" he continued.

"Exactly!" agreed Robina.

His Holiness nodded. "Most people think that their only option is to change their circumstances. But these are not the true causes of their unhappiness. It has more to do with the way they think about their circumstances."

"We encourage our students to turn their jails into monasteries," said Robina. "To stop thinking about their time inside as a waste of their life and instead to see it as an amazing opportunity for personal growth. There are some who do, and the transformation in those people is incredible. They are able to find real meaning and purpose, and they come out as completely changed people."

"Very good," His Holiness said, smiling warmly. "It would be wonderful if everyone could hear that message—especially those who live in jails of their own making."

As he made that point, the Dalai Lama looked over at me, but I didn't know why. I had never for a moment imagined that I was a prisoner. Snow Lion—yes. The Most Beautiful Creature That Ever Lived—certainly! Of course, I did have some problems, being a single cat the biggest of them.

But prisoner?

Me?

It was only much later that His Holiness's meaning became clear. After the visitors had departed, the Dalai Lama asked to see Mrs. Trinci to thank her for the meal.

"It was wonderful," he enthused. "Your dessert in particular. Venerable Robina liked it very much. I hope it wasn't too stressful to prepare?"

"Oh, no—*non troppo!* Not much."

In His Holiness's presence, Mrs. Trinci was a changed woman. The towering Brunhilde from one of Tenzin's Wagnerian operas, who dominated the kitchen, was nowhere to be seen, replaced instead by a blushing schoolgirl.

"We don't want you to have too much stress." The Dalai Lama looked at her thoughtfully for a moment before telling her, "It was a very interesting lunch. We were saying how happiness, contentment—this does not depend on circumstance. Mrs. Trinci, you are single and you seem happy to me."

"I don't want another husband," declared Mrs. Trinci, "if that's what you mean."

"So being single is not the cause of unhappiness?"

"No, no! *Mia vita è buona.* My life is good. I am very fulfilled."

His Holiness nodded. "I feel the same."

At that moment, I knew what the Dalai Lama meant about prisons of our own making. He hadn't been talking only about physical circumstances but also about the ideas and beliefs we have that make us unhappy. In my own case, it was the idea that I needed another cat's company to be happy.

Mrs. Trinci walked toward the door as though to leave. But before opening it, she hesitated. "May I ask you a question, Your Holiness?"

"Of course."

"I have been coming here to cook for more than twenty years, but you have never tried to convert me. Why is that?"

"What a funny thing to say, Mrs. Trinci!" His Holiness burst out laughing. Taking her hand gently in his, he told her, "The purpose of Buddhism is not to convert people. It is to give them tools so they can create greater happiness. So they can be happier Catholics, happier atheists, happier Buddhists. There are many practices, and I know you are already very familiar with one of them."

Mrs. Trinci raised her eyebrows.

"It is the wonderful paradox," he continued, "that the best way to achieve happiness for oneself is to give happiness to others."

That evening I sat on my windowsill, looking out across the temple courtyard. I would try an experiment, I decided. Next time I caught myself yearning for another cat in my life, I would remind myself of His Holiness and Mrs. Trinci, who were both very contentedly single. I would deliberately set about making some other being happy, even if it was as simple as bestowing a kindly purr, in order to shift the focus of my thoughts off myself and onto others. I would explore the "wonderful paradox" the Dalai Lama spoke about to see if it worked for me.

Even in the act of making this decision I found myself unaccountably lighter—feeling less burdened and more carefree. It was not my circumstances that were causing me distress but my belief about these circumstances. By letting go of the unhappiness-creating belief that I needed another cat, I would convert my jail into a monastery.

I was contemplating this very thought when something caught my eye—a movement next to a large rock in the flower bed on the other side of the courtyard.

Darkness had already fallen, but the rock was illuminated by a green light that burned all night on a nearby market stall. For a long while I paused, staring across the distance.

No, I wasn't mistaken! Transfixed, I began to make out the silhouette: large, leonine, like a wild beast that had emerged from the jungle, with watchful dark eyes and perfectly symmetrical stripes. A magnificent tiger tabby.

With fluid grace he slipped onto the rock, his movement purposeful and mesmerizing. From there he surveyed Jokhang, as a landowner might survey the far pavilions of his empire, before his head turned to the window where I sat. And paused.

I held his gaze.

There was no obvious acknowledgment of my presence. He had seen me, I was sure, but what was he thinking? Who could tell? He gave away nothing at all.

He stayed on the rock for only a moment before he was gone, disappearing into the undergrowth as mysteriously as he'd come.

In the falling darkness, squares of light appeared in the windows of Namgyal Monastery as the monks returned to their rooms.

The night seemed alive with possibility.

CHAPTER THREE

Can you become famous by association?

Although I had never asked the question, I discovered the answer within a few months of arriving in McLeod Ganj, on the outskirts of Dharamsala. My ventures into the outside world had become bolder and more frequent, as I became familiar not only with the Dalai Lama's quarters and the temple complex but also with the world down the hill from Jokhang.

Immediately outside the temple gates were stalls selling fruit, snacks, and other fresh produce, mainly to the locals. There were also a few stalls for tourists, the biggest and most resplendent being "S. J. Patel's Quality International Budget Tours." The proprietor carried the widest range of goods and services, from local tours around Dharamsala to trips to Nepal. At his stall, visitors could also buy maps, umbrellas, mobile phones, batteries, and bottles of water. From early in the morning until long after the other stalls had closed, Mr. Patel could be seen hustling tourists for trade, gesticulating excitedly as he spoke into his mobile phone or, from time to time, dozing in the reclined passenger seat of his pride and joy, a 1972 Mercedes that was parked nearby.

Neither Mr. Patel nor the other stall holders had much to interest a cat, so it wasn't long before I ventured farther down the street. There I found a clutch of small shops, one of which immediately had my nostrils twitching with the bouquet of enticing aromas that wafted from its doors.

Flower boxes, sidewalk tables, and jaunty yellow-and-red umbrellas bedecked with auspicious Tibetan symbols lined the entrance to Café Franc, a brasserie from which emanated the scents of baking bread and freshly ground coffee, interlaced with even more appetizing suggestions of fish pie, pâté, and mouthwatering Mornay sauce.

From a flower bed opposite the restaurant, I observed the ebb and swell of tourists who frequented the outside tables each day: the earnest hikers gathering around their laptops and smartphones, planning expeditions, sharing photographs, and speaking on crackling connections to the folks back home; the spiritual tourists visiting India in search of mystical experiences; the celebrity hunters who had come here hoping for a photograph of the Dalai Lama.

One man seemed to spend most of his time at the place. Early in the morning he would pull up outside in a bright red Fiat Punto, incongruously new and polished for a ramshackle street in McLeod Ganj. Springing from the driver's door, his head entirely bald and polished, his clothing tight, black, and stylish, he was closely followed by a French bulldog. The two strutted into the café as though taking to the stage. During different visits I noticed the man both inside and out, sometimes barking orders at waiters, sometimes sitting at a table poring over papers while keying numbers into a glistening black smartphone.

I can't, dear reader, explain why I didn't work out immediately who he was, or where his cat-versus-dog proclivities lay, or the evident folly of venturing any closer to Café Franc. But the truth is, I was naïve to all this, perhaps because, at the time, I was little more than a kitten.

The afternoon of my fateful visit, the chef at Café Franc had prepared a particularly enticing *plat du jour*. The aroma of roast chicken wafted all the way up to the gates of the temple—an invocation I found impossible to resist. Padding down the hill as fast as my unsteady gait would allow, it wasn't long before I was standing directly beside one of the boxes of scarlet geraniums at the entrance.

With no strategy beyond a vain hope that my mere presence would be enough to conjure up a generous serving of lunch—it seemed to work with Mrs. Trinci—I ventured toward one of the tables. The four backpackers sitting there were too intent on their cheeseburgers to pay me the least attention.

I must do more.

At a table farther inside, an older, Mediterranean-looking man glanced at me with complete indifference as he sipped his black coffee.

By now quite far inside the restaurant, I was wondering where to go next when suddenly there was a growl.

The French bulldog, only a matter of yards away, stared at me menacingly. What I should have done was nothing at all. Held my ground. Hissed wrathfully. Treated the dog with such lofty disdain that it didn't dare come a step closer.

But I was a young and foolish kitten, so I took off, which only provoked the beast further. There was a thundering of paws as it bolted across the wooden floor toward me. A flailing of limbs as I scampered as fast as my legs would allow. Sudden, hideous growling as it bore down on me. Panic and pandemonium as I found myself cornered in the unfamiliar room. My heart was beating so fast I felt I would explode. Ahead of me was an old-fashioned newspaper rack with some space behind it. With no other option and the beast so close I could smell its foul, sulfuric breath, I was forced to jump up and over the rack, landing on the floor on the other side with a thud.

Victory snatched so abruptly from its jaws, the dog went berserk. It could see me only inches away but couldn't get closer. As it yapped hysterically, human voices were raised.

"Huge rat!" exclaimed one.

"Over there!" cried another.

In moments, a black shadow loomed above me, along with the powerful scent of Kouros aftershave.

Next I felt a curious sensation, one I hadn't experienced since life as a newborn kitten. A tightening around the neck, the sense of being lifted. Picked up by the scruff, I found myself looking at the shiny bald pate and baleful hazel eyes of Franc, into whose café I had trespassed and whose French bulldog I had enraged and who—most important of all—was evidently no lover of cats.

Time stood still. Enough for me to observe the anger in those bulging eyes, the pulsing blue vein that ran up to his temple, the clenched jaw and pursed lips, the glittering gold Om symbol that dangled from his left ear.

"A cat!" he spat, as though the very idea of it was an affront. Looking down at the bulldog, he said, "Marcel! How could you let this . . . thing in here?" His accent was American, his tone indignant.

Marcel slunk away, cowed.

Franc strode to the front of the brasserie. He was clearly going to eject me. And the idea suddenly filled me with terror. Most cats are capable of leaping from great heights without the least harm. But I am not most cats. My hind legs were already weak and unstable. Further impact could cause them irreparable harm. What if I could never walk again? What if I could never find my way back to Jokhang?!

The Mediterranean man still sat impassively with his coffee. The backpackers were bent over their plates, shoving French fries into their mouths. No one was about to come to my rescue.

Franc's expression was implacable as he made his way to the roadside. He lifted me higher. He drew his arm back. He was preparing not simply to drop me but to launch me like a missile into the street beyond his premises.

This was when two monks walked past on their way up to Jokhang. Catching sight of me, they folded their hands at their hearts and bowed slightly.

Franc swung around to see who was behind him. But finding no lama or holy man, he looked curiously at the monks.

"The Dalai Lama's cat," one of them explained.

"Very good karma," his companion added.

A group of monks coming along behind them repeated the bowing.

"You're sure?" Franc was astonished.

"His Holiness's Cat," they chorused.

The change that overcame Franc was immediate and total. Drawing me to his chest, he placed me carefully on his other arm and began stroking me with the hand that only moments before had been poised to throw me. Back into Café Franc we went, crossing to a section where a display of English-language newspapers and magazines lent a cosmopolitan flair to the establishment. On a broad shelf, there was an empty space between *The Times* of London and *The Wall Street Journal*. It was here that Franc placed me, as delicately as if I were a very fine piece of Ming dynasty porcelain.

"Warm milk," he ordered from a passing waiter. "And some of today's chicken. Chop, chop!"

Then, as Marcel trotted over, baring his teeth, his owner warned, "And if *you* so much as *look* at this little darling"—Franc raised his index finger—"it'll be *Indian* dog food for you tonight!"

The chicken duly arrived and was every bit as delicious as it had smelled. Recharged and reassured of my newfound status, I climbed from the lowest shelf on the rack to the highest, finding a congenial niche between *Vanity Fair* and *Vogue*. It was a position more appropriate to the Snow Lion of Jokhang, not to mention one that afforded a much better view of the brasserie.

Café Franc was a truly Himalayan hybrid—metropolitan chic meets Buddhist mystique. Along with the glossy magazine rack, espresso machine, and elegant table settings, it was decorated with Buddha statues, *thangkas*, and ritual objects, like the inside of a temple. One wall featured gilt-framed black-and-white photographs of Franc: Franc presenting a white scarf to the Dalai Lama; Franc being blessed by the Karmapa; Franc standing next to Richard Gere; Franc at the entrance to Tiger's Nest Monastery in Bhutan. Patrons could gaze at these while a hypnotic musical arrangement of the Tibetan Buddhist chant "Om Mani Padme Hum" emerged from the speakers.

As I settled in my newfound aerie, I followed the comings and goings with keen interest. When I was noticed by a pair of American girls who began cooing and stroking me, Franc crossed over to them. "The Dalai Lama's cat," he murmured.

"Omigod!" they squealed.

He gave a world-weary shrug. "Comes in all the time."

"Omigod!" they squealed again. "What's her name?"

His expression went blank for a moment before he recovered. "Rinpoche," he told them. "It means precious. A very special title usually only given to lamas."

"Omigod! Can we, like, take a photograph with her?"

"No flash." Franc was stern. "Rinpoche must not be disturbed."

The pattern was repeated throughout the day. "Dalai Lama's cat," he would say, indicating my presence with a nod of the head as he handed customers their bills. "Adores our roast chicken." To others, he would add, "We take care of her for His Holiness. Isn't she divine?"

41

"Talk about karma," he liked to point out. "Rinpoche. It means precious."

At home, I was HHC, treated with much love by the Dalai Lama and great kindness by his staff, but I was a cat nonetheless. At Café Franc, however, I was a celebrity! At home, I was given cat biscuits at lunchtime, proclaimed by the manufacturers to provide growing kittens with fully balanced nutrition. At Café Franc, beef bourguignon, coq au vin, and lamb Provençal were the daily fare, offered up to where I sat on a lotus cushion Franc soon installed for my comfort. It wasn't long before I forsook the biscuits at Jokhang in favor of regular visits to Café Franc unless the weather was inclement.

Quite apart from the food, Café Franc turned out to be the most wonderful entertainment venue. The aroma of roasted, organic coffee exerted a magnetic spell on Western visitors to McLeod Ganj of every age, temperament, and coloring imaginable, who arrived speaking a great variety of languages and wearing the most astonishing range of clothing. After spending all my short life surrounded by soft-spoken monks in saffron and red, visiting Café Franc was like visiting the zoo.

But it wasn't long before I began to realize that beneath all the apparent differences, there were many more ways in which the tourists were quite similar. One way, in particular, I found intriguing.

On days when Mrs. Trinci wasn't in the kitchen, food preparation up the hill was always uncomplicated. Most meals were rice- or noodle-based, garnished with vegetables, fish, or, less often, meat. This was the case in both the Dalai Lama's household and the nearby monastery kitchens, where huge vats of rice or vegetable stew were stirred by novices wielding broom-length ladles. But although the ingredients were basic, meal times were occasions of great enjoyment and relish. The monks would eat slowly, in companionable silence, savoring every mouthful. There would be an occasional observation about the flavor of a spice or the texture of the rice. From the expressions on their faces, it was as though they were on a journey of discovery: what sensory pleasure awaited them today? What nuance would they find that was subtly different or gratifying?

A short wobble down the road at Café Franc it was a different universe. From my lookout on the top shelf of the magazine rack, I could see directly through the glass panel of the kitchen door. From well before dawn, two Nepalese brothers, Jigme and Ngawang Dragpa, were hard at work baking croissants, *pain au chocolat*, and all manner of pastries, as well as sourdough, French, Italian, and Turkish breads.

· The moment the café doors opened at 7 A.M., the Dragpa brothers launched into a breakfast service that included eggs—fried, poached, scrambled, boiled, Benedict, Florentine, or in omelets—as well as hash brown potatoes, bacon, *chipolatas*, mushrooms, tomatoes, and French toast, not to mention a buffet of muesli and cereals and fruit juices, accompanied by a full range of teas and barista-made coffees. At 11 A.M., breakfast would segue into lunch, which demanded an entirely new menu of even greater complexity, and that, in turn, was succeeded by an even more diverse range of dishes for dinner.

Never had I seen such variety of foods, prepared to such exacting standards, with ingredients from every continent. The handful of spice jars in the monastery kitchen seemed altogether inadequate when compared with the multiple racks of spices, sauces, condiments, and flavorings in the kitchen of Café Franc.

If the monks up the hill were able to find such pleasure in the most basic of foods, surely the delectable cuisine offered to patrons of Café Franc should be the cause of the most intensely spine-tingling, claw-curling, whisker-quivering ecstasy imaginable?

As it happened, no.

After the first few mouthfuls, most customers at Café Franc hardly noticed their food or coffee. Despite all the elaborate preparations, for which they paid a high price, they virtually ignored their food, too busily engaged in conversation, or texting friends and relatives, or reading one of the foreign newspapers Franc collected daily from the post office.

I found it bewildering. It was almost as if they didn't know *how* to eat.

Many of these same tourists stayed in hotels that provided coffee- and tea-making equipment in their rooms. If they wanted to drink a cup of coffee without actually experiencing it, why didn't they do it for free back at the hotel? Why pay $3 to *not* drink a cup of coffee at Café Franc?

It was His Holiness's two executive assistants who helped me make sense of what was happening. Sitting in the room they shared the morning following my first visit to Café Franc, I looked up as Chogyal pushed back from his desk. "I like this definition of mindfulness," he said to Tenzin, reading from one of the many manuscripts received each week from authors petitioning His Holiness to write a foreword. "'Mindfulness means paying attention to the present moment deliberately and non-judgmentally.' Nice and clear, isn't it?"

Tenzin nodded.

"Not dwelling on thoughts of the past or the future, or some kind of fantasy," elaborated Chogyal.

"I like an even simpler definition by Sogyal Rinpoche," said Tenzin, sitting back in his chair. "Pure presence."

"Hmm," Chogyal mused. "No mental agitation or elaboration of any kind."

"Exactly," confirmed Tenzin. "The foundation of all contentment."

On my next visit to Café Franc, having enjoyed a hearty helping of Scottish smoked salmon with a side of double-thick clotted cream—a meal I can assure you that I ate with the most intense, if somewhat noisy, mindfulness—I settled onto the lotus-pattern cushion between the latest issues of the fashion magazines and continued my observation of the clientele.

And the more I observed, the more obvious it became: what was missing was mindfulness. Even though they were sitting a few hundred yards from the Dalai Lama's headquarters, in the Tibetan Buddhist theme park that was Café Franc, rather than experiencing this unique place and moment, most of the time they were mentally far, far away.

Moving between Jokhang and Café Franc more and more often, I began to see that up the hill, happiness was sought by cultivating inner qualities, beginning with mindfulness but also including such things as generosity, equanimity, and a good heart. Down the hill, happiness was sought from external things—restaurant food, stimulating holidays, and lightning-quick technology. There seemed to be no reason, however, that humans couldn't have both: we cats knew that being mindful of delicious food was among the greatest happinesses imaginable!

One day an interesting couple appeared at Café Franc. At first glance, they were quite ordinary-looking, middle-aged Americans in jeans and sweatshirts. They arrived during a midmorning lull, and Franc sashayed over to their table in his new black Emporio Armani jeans.

"And how are we this morning?" he asked, in his standard opener.

As Franc took their coffee orders, the man asked about the colored strings around his wrist, and Franc began the recitation with which I was now familiar: "They're blessing strings, and you get them from a lama when you take special initiations. The red one was from the Kalachakra initiations I took from the Dalai Lama in two thousand eight. The blue ones are from vajrayana initiations in Boulder, San Francisco, and New York, in two thousand six, two thousand eight, and two thousand ten. I got the yellow ones at empowerments in Melbourne, Scotland, and Goa."

"Very interesting," replied the man.

"Oh, the Dharma is my life," Franc announced, placing a theatrical hand over his heart, then nodding his head in my direction. "Have you seen our little friend? The Dalai Lama's cat. In here all the time. Close karmic connection to His Holiness." Then, leaning closer, he confided, as he did at least a dozen times a day, "We're at the heart of Tibetan Buddhism here. The absolute epicenter!"

Quite what the couple made of Franc was hard to tell. But what set them apart from other visitors was that when their coffee was placed in front of them, they stopped their conversation and actually tasted it. Not only the first mouthful but also the second, third, and subsequent mouthfuls. Like the monks at Jokhang, they were paying attention to the present moment deliberately. Relishing their coffee. Enjoying their surroundings. Experiencing pure presence.

Which was why, when they resumed conversation, I eavesdropped with particular interest. What I heard should not have surprised me. The man, a researcher in mindfulness from America, was telling his wife about an article that had appeared in the *Harvard Gazette*.

"They used a panel of more than two thousand people with smartphones and sent out questions at random intervals during the week. Always they were the same three questions: *What are you doing? What are you thinking? How happy are you?* What they found was that forty-seven percent of the time, people weren't thinking about what they were doing."

His wife raised her eyebrows.

"Personally, I think that number is a bit low," he said. "Half the time, people aren't focusing on what they're doing. But the really interesting bit is the correlation with happiness. They found that people are much happier when they're mindful of what they're doing."

"Because they only pay attention to things they enjoy?" asked his wife.

He shook his head. "That's just it. Turns out that it's not so much *what* you're doing that makes you happy. It's whether or not you're being mindful of what you're doing. The important thing is to be in the direct state, attending to the here and now. Not in the narrative state"—he spun his index finger beside his temple—"which means thinking about anything except what you're actually doing."

"That's what Buddhists have always said," agreed his wife.

Her husband nodded. "Only sometimes these concepts get lost in translation. You come across people like the maître d' here, who wears Buddhism like a badge. For them it's an extension of their ego, a way to present themselves as different or special. They seem to think it's all about the external trappings, when in fact the only thing that really matters is inner transformation."

A few weeks later, I was enjoying a post-luncheon doze on the top shelf when I awoke to a face that was as deeply familiar as it was completely out of context. Tenzin was standing in the middle of Café Franc, looking directly at me.

"You've noticed our beautiful visitor?" Franc glanced over at me.

"Oh yes. Very pretty." In his tailored suit, the ambassadorial Tenzin gave away nothing.

"The Dalai Lama's cat."

"Really?"

"Comes in here all the time."

"Amazing!" The usual carbolic tang of Tenzin's fingers intermingled with a potent dose of Kouros as he reached up to scratch my chin.

"She has a very close karmic connection to His Holiness," Franc told His Holiness's right-hand man.

"I'm sure you're right," Tenzin mused, before posing a question that Franc had not yet considered. "I wonder if she is missed by His Holiness's household when she comes visiting?"

"I doubt it very much," Franc returned smoothly. "But if they found her here, they'd soon realize how well she's looked after."

"That *is* a nice cushion."

"Not just the cushion, dear. It's lunch that she enjoys."

"Hungry, is she?"

"Loves her food. *Adores* her food."

"Perhaps she doesn't get enough food at Jokhang?" Tenzin suggested.

"I'm sure it's not that. It's just that Rinpoche has particular tastes."

"*Rinpoche?*" Tenzin wore a droll expression.

"That's her name." Franc had said it so many times now that he had actually come to believe it. "And you can see why, can't you?"

"As the Dharma tells us"—Tenzin's reply was cryptic—"*everything* depends on mind."

Back at home several afternoons later, Tenzin sat opposite His Holiness in the familiar office. It was something of a ritual at the end of the working day—Tenzin updating His Holiness on any matter of importance and the two of them talking about what needed to be done, while enjoying freshly brewed cups of green tea.

I was on my usual windowsill, watching the sun slip below the horizon and only half-listening to their discussion, which ranged, as usual, from global geopolitics to the finer points of esoteric Buddhist philosophy.

"Oh, Your Holiness, turning to more important matters"—Tenzin closed the United Nations file in front of him—"I'm pleased to tell you that I've solved the mystery of HHC's eating disorder."

A glint appeared in the Dalai Lama's eyes as he responded to Tenzin's expression. "Please"— he leaned back in his chair—"go on."

"It seems that our little Snow Lion isn't losing her appetite after all. Instead, she's been taking herself down the road to the brasserie run by our designer-Buddhist friend."

"Brasserie?"

"Just down the road," he gestured. "With the red-and-yellow umbrellas outside."

"Oh, yes. I know the place." His Holiness nodded. "I hear they have very good food. I'm surprised she hasn't moved there!"

"As it happens, the owner is very much a dog lover."

"He is?"

"He has some special breed."

"But he also feeds our little one?"

"Reveres her because he knows she lives with you."

His Holiness chuckled.

"Not only that, he's given her the name Rinpoche."

"*Rinpoche*?" It was too much for the Dalai Lama, who burst out laughing.

"Yes," said Tenzin as they both turned to look at me. "Funny name to call a cat."

A late afternoon breeze brought the scent of Himalayan pine through the open window.

His Holiness's expression was thoughtful. "But perhaps not such a bad name if she has helped the restaurant owner develop more equanimity for dogs *and* cats. For him, therefore, she *is* precious."

Rising from his chair, he came over to stroke me. "You know, Tenzin, sometimes if I am working at my desk for a long time, our little Snow Lion will come and rub against my legs. Sometimes," he chortled, "she will even bite my ankles until I stop what I'm doing. She wants me to pick her up and say hello and spend a few moments being together, just the two of us.

"For me," he continued, "she is a beautiful reminder to be in this moment, here and now. What could be more precious? So I suppose"—he looked at me with that oceanic love—"she is my Rinpoche, too."

CHAPTER FOUR

It was an overcast and unpromising day when I ventured out of the Dalai Lama's office into that of his executive assistants. It so happened that both Chogyal and Tenzin were away from their desks, but the office wasn't completely unattended.

There, curled up in a wicker basket by the radiator, was a Lhasa apso.

For those unfamiliar with the breed, Lhasa apsos are small, long-haired dogs who, in the past, helped to guard the monasteries of Tibet. They have a special place in the affections of Tibetans—sometimes from my sill I watch visitors down below circumambulating the temple with their Lhasa apsos, an auspicious ritual believed to help achieve higher rebirth. But discovering one so close to my own inner sanctum came as a most unwelcome surprise.

Dozing in its basket as I entered the room, the dog raised its nose and sniffed the air before deciding to play it safe and bury its furry head back in its basket. For my part, I walked past without so much as acknowledging its existence, hopping up onto Chogyal's desk and from there to my favorite viewing platform on top of the wooden filing cabinet.

Moments later, Chogyal returned. Leaning down, he patted the small dog and talked to him in the familiar and endearing tone of voice I'd always thought he reserved for me. As my hackles rose, the betrayal only deepened. Oblivious to my presence, Chogyal spent quite some time stroking and caressing the beast—which looked a very scrawny specimen—reassuring it of its good looks, its delightful temperament, and the special care he was going to give it. The very same sentiments he usually whispered in my ear—and which I'd always imagined were sincere and heartfelt. Listening to him repeat those words to this dull-eyed, lank-haired interloper made me realize that far from being exclusive, they were just stock phrases he repeated to any creature with four legs and a furry face.

So much for our special relationship!

Chogyal resumed his place at the desk, tapping away on his keyboard, not realizing that I was sitting only yards away and had seen everything. When Tenzin arrived about 20 minutes later, he too acknowledged the dog by name—Kyi Kyi, pronounced with a long "i," as in "kite"—before sitting at his own desk.

I found it hard to believe that they both could sit there reading and replying to e-mails as though nothing out of the ordinary was happening. Matters only got worse when the Dalai Lama's translator arrived with a newly completed manuscript under his arm. Lobsang was tall, slender, and youthful, and tranquility seemed to ooze from his every pore. I had believed myself to be a favorite of his, but he too bent to stroke the new arrival before crossing to greet me.

"And how is our little Snow Lion today?" He began tickling under my chin before I seized his fingers in the steel-vise-grip of my teeth.

"I didn't realize she'd met our special guest," Chogyal said, looking up at me with his usual smile, as if I were supposed to be as pleased as he was.

"Not necessarily *her* special guest," observed Tenzin. Turning to look directly at me, he added, "But hopefully you can find a place in your heart for Kyi Kyi."

Eyes darkening with displeasure, I released Lobsang's hand and descended to the desk, then the floor, and stalked out of the room, ears pressed back. The Dalai Lama's three staffers seemed not to notice.

At lunchtime, I observed Chogyal taking the dog for a walk. It trotted obediently beside him as they circumambulated the temple, and there was much stopping and petting by admiring Tibetans as they came and went from the temple complex.

In the kitchen, Chogyal fed us both at the regular time. But it was hard to avoid comparing the huge mound of food heaped on Kyi Kyi's plate with my customarily modest portion. Or the fact that Chogyal stayed to watch over the dog as it wolfed down its meal, making a great fuss over it and giving it a rewarding pat afterward, while leaving me to my own devices.

When we bumped into His Holiness in the corridor later, he too crouched down to say hello to the dog. "So this is Kyi Kyi?" he confirmed, patting the dog with much more warmth than I would have liked. "Beautiful markings! Such a handsome little chap!"

They were all making such a big deal you'd have thought they'd never seen a Lhasa apso before! And despite the chatter, none of my questions were being answered—like, what was the dog doing here? And how long would it stay?

It was my ardent hope that the Dalai Lama wasn't planning to adopt it. There wasn't room in this relationship for the three of us.

But the next day when I ventured out, Kyi Kyi was there again in his basket.

And the day after that.

This was why another, rather more high-powered visitor that week came as a welcome distraction.

The whole of McLeod Ganj knew that someone special was arriving when a huge, black Range Rover rolled ponderously up the hill toward Jokhang. Locals and tourists alike stared at the high-polished, expensive, and expansive apparition, so out of keeping with the town that it might have materialized from a different planet. Exactly who was behind those dark-tinted windows? What did you have to do to be conveyed about with such extravagant secrecy?

One question that didn't need to be asked, however, was who the visitor had come to see. And sure enough, the Range Rover eventually made its slow way through the gates toward the home of Rinpoche, the Bodhicatva, the Snow Lion of Jokhang, The Most Beautiful Creature That Ever Lived—and her human companion.

I recognized the visitor from the moment he stepped into His Holiness's room. He was, after all, one of the most famous and longest-established self-development gurus in the world. His face was emblazoned on the covers of millions of books and DVDs. He had toured world capitals, speaking to huge crowds in the cities' largest venues. He had a personal following among the Hollywood in-crowd, he had met with U.S. presidents, and he appeared regularly on every major TV talk show.

However, my deep sense of discretion prevents me from telling you who he was—no, really, especially in light of the combustible revelations he was about to make, which he certainly didn't intend for a wider audience. The moment he stepped through the door, his presence was commanding. It was as if the very fact that he was there obliged you to look at him.

Of course, the Dalai Lama has a powerful presence, too—but of an altogether different nature. In His Holiness's case, it's not so much a personal presence as an encounter with Goodness. From the time you are first with him, you become absorbed in a state of being in which all your normal thoughts and concerns fade into irrelevance, and you become aware, in a curious way *reminded*, that your own essential nature is one of boundless love and that this being the case, all is well.

Our guest—let's just call him Jack—strode into the room, presented His Holiness with a scarf in the traditional way, and was soon sitting beside him in the wingback chair reserved for visitors. These were the very same actions performed by most visitors, but the way Jack did them made them seem somehow more potent, as though his every word, every gesture, was imbued with significance. Their conversation began with the usual pleasantries, then Jack gave His Holiness a copy of his latest book. As he told the Dalai Lama about his world tour a year earlier, he was mesmerizing. As he described a movie in which he had recently appeared, it was easy to imagine Jack's on-screen charisma.

But after ten minutes, conversation gave way to silence. His Holiness sat in his chair, relaxed, attentive, a gentle smile on his face. It seemed that for all of Jack's powerful self-assurance, he was finding it hard to get to the point of why he had come here. Eventually he started to speak again—but as he did, something extraordinary started to unfold.

"Your Holiness, as you may know, I have been working as a life coach for more than twenty years. I've helped millions of people around the world find their passions, realize their dreams, and lead lives of success and abundance." The words came to him with effortless familiarity, but as he spoke, something about him was changing. Something I found hard to identify.

"I've helped people find fulfillment in every aspect of their lives, not just material." Jack continued. "I've motivated them to develop their unique talents and abilities. To create successful relationships."

With every sentence, he seemed to be losing some of his polish. He was shrinking, almost physically, into his chair.

"I have created the largest self-development company in America, possibly in the world." He said it almost as an admission of failure. "In the process, I've become a very successful and wealthy man."

This last sentence had the greatest impact of all. In giving voice to the accomplishment of all that he had set out to achieve, he also seemed to be confessing just how poorly it had served him. He leaned forward, shoulders rounded and elbows on his knees. He looked broken. When he gazed up at His Holiness, it was with an imploring expression.

"But it isn't working for me."

His Holiness regarded him sympathetically.

"On our last world tour, I was making a quarter of a million dollars every single night. We'd packed the biggest indoor venues across America. But I'd never felt so hollow. Motivating people to be wealthy and successful and in great relationships suddenly seemed so senseless. It may have been my dream once, but not anymore.

"I went home and told everyone I needed a break. I stopped going into work. I grew a beard. I spent lots of time at home just reading and looking after the garden. My wife, Bree, didn't like that. She still wanted to spend weekends with celebrities, and party and appear in the social pages. At first, she thought I was having a midlife crisis. Then things got acrimonious. Our relationship grew worse and worse, until she said she wanted a divorce. That was three months ago. Right now, I'm so confused I don't know what to do.

"And you know the worst part? I actually feel bad that I feel bad. Everyone out there believes that I'm living the dream. They imagine that my life is incredibly fulfilled and happy. I encouraged them to think that, because I really believed it was true. But I was wrong. It isn't true. It never was."

The commanding authority had evaporated, the charisma had dissolved, leaving only this sad, crumpled man. It was impossible not to feel sorry for Jack. The difference between the persona he projected and the man being revealed could not have been greater. Seen from the outside, his wealth and fame and guru status might appear to equip him to deal with life's problems far better than most. But if anything, the opposite now seemed true.

His Holiness leaned forward in his seat. "I am sorry that what you are experiencing is so painful. But there is another way of looking at it. What you are going through now is very useful. Perhaps later you will see this as the best thing that has ever happened to you. Dissatisfaction with the material world is—what do you say?—vital to spiritual development."

The notion that his present unhappiness was somehow useful took Jack by surprise. But the Dalai Lama's response also troubled him. "You're not saying there's something wrong with wealth, are you?"

"Oh no," said His Holiness. "Wealth is a form of power, an energy. It can be most beneficial when used for good purposes. But, as you see, it is not a true cause of happiness. Some of the happiest people I know have very little money."

"What about fulfilling our unique abilities?" Jack turned to another of his former beliefs. "Are you saying that's not a cause of happiness either?"

The Dalai Lama smiled. "We all have certain predispositions. Some particular strengths. Cultivating these abilities can be very helpful. But—same with money—what matters is not the abilities themselves but how we use them."

"What about romance and love?" By now, Jack was scraping the bottom of the barrel of his former creed, and his own skepticism showed.

"You have a happy relationship with your wife for a long time?"

"Eighteen years."

"And then"—His Holiness turned the palms of his hands upward—"change. Impermanence. It is the nature of all things, especially relationships. They are certainly not a true cause of happiness."

"When you say 'true cause,' what do you mean?"

"A cause that can be relied upon. One that always works. Heat applied to water is a true cause of steam. No matter who applies the heat or how often the heat has been applied before or where in the world heat is applied, the result is always steam. In the case of money or status or relationships"—His Holiness chuckled—"we can easily see these are not true causes of happiness."

While the self-evident truth of what the Dalai Lama had just said confirmed Jack's own experience, the simplicity and clarity with which he had said it seemed to startle our visitor. "To think that all these years I've been preaching the Gospel of Self-Development, but I've had it so wrong."

"You should not be too harsh on yourself," said His Holiness. "If you help people lead more positive lives that benefit others as well as themselves, this is a good thing. Very good thing. The danger is that self-development can lead us to more self-cherishing, self-absorption, self-infatuation. And these are not true causes of happiness but the opposite."

Jack took a moment to process this before asking, "So, the true causes of happiness. Do we need to discover what these are for ourselves, or are there general principles? Must we turn our back on the material world?"

He didn't get any further before the Dalai Lama began laughing. "Oh, no!" he said. "Becoming a monk is not a true cause of happiness either!" Then, adopting a more serious expression, he continued, "We each need to find out our own personal methods of cultivating happiness, but there *are* general principles. Two main true causes of happiness: first, the wish to give happiness to others, which Buddhists define as love, and second, the wish to help free others from dissatisfaction or suffering, which we define as compassion.

"The main shift, you see, is from placing *self* at the center of our thoughts to putting *others* there. It is—what do you say?—a paradox that the more we can focus our thoughts on the well-being of others, the happier we become. The first one to benefit is oneself. I call this being wisely selfish."

"An interesting philosophy," mused Jack. "Wisely selfish."

"We should test these principles against our own experience to see if they are true," His Holiness said. "For example, think of the times in your life when you experienced great contentment. Perhaps you find that your thoughts were on someone else. Then compare. Think about your times of greatest unhappiness, upset. Who were you thinking about then?"

As his visitor was considering this, His Holiness continued, "Scientific research is most useful. MRI scans have been done on meditators while they're focusing on different subjects. We expect the meditators to have greatest happiness when their minds are completely calm and relaxed. But the prefrontal cortex of the brain, the part linked to positive emotion, lights up when people meditate on the happiness of others. Therefore, the more 'other-centric' we are, the happier we can be:"

Jack was nodding. "Self-Development takes us only so far. Then there needs to be Other Development."

The Dalai Lama brought his hands together with a smile. "Exactly."

Jack paused before saying, "Now I understand why you said that something useful can come from this experience."

"There is a story, a metaphor, that perhaps you may find useful," said His Holiness. "A man arrives home to find a huge pile of sheep manure has been dumped on his front yard. He didn't order the manure. He does not want it. But somehow, it is there, and his only choice now is to decide what to do with it. He can put it in his pockets and walk around all day complaining to everyone about what happened. But if he does this, people will start avoiding him after a while. *More* useful is if he spreads the manure on his garden.

"We all face this same choice when dealing with problems. We don't ask for them. We don't want them. But the way we deal with them is what's most important. If we are wise, the greatest problems can lead to the greatest insights."

Later that day, I was in my usual spot in the executive assistants' office. Remembering Jack's arrival that morning, I continued to be amazed by how powerfully he filled the room when he first stepped through the door—and how very different he seemed when he was telling the Dalai Lama how he really felt. The difference between appearance and reality could not have been more marked. I also reflected on His Holiness's advice about how to deal with problems in life. They are never asked for, but how we deal with them defines our future happiness or unhappiness.

Toward the end of that afternoon, the Dalai Lama's driver appeared in the office. It was more than a week since he had last visited, and he immediately noticed the Lhasa apso, who lay curled up in his basket.

"Who is this?" he asked Chogyal, who was tidying his desk in readiness to leave for the day.

"Just someone we're looking after until a home can be found for him."

"Another Tibetan refugee?" wisecracked the driver, leaning down to pat the dog.

"Similar," said Chogyal. "He belonged to neighbors of my cousin in Dharamsala. They had him only a few weeks, and my cousin kept hearing this yelping coming from their yard.

"Then about a week ago, my cousin heard the dog barking from inside the house at night. He went around and knocked on the door. No one answered, but the barking stopped. Next night, the same thing. He began to wonder what was going on. It seemed the neighbors weren't taking good care of the dog."

The driver shook his head.

"Two days later, my cousin happened to mention the dog to the neighbor across the road, who told him that the dog's owners had moved out the weekend before. Cleared out, lock, stock, and barrel."

"And abandoned the puppy?" asked the driver.

Chogyal nodded. "My cousin went around immediately and broke into the house. He found Kyi Kyi lying at the end of a heavy chain in the kitchen, barely alive. It was a pitiful sight. No food or water. He took the dog home immediately and managed to get some water into him, then food. But my cousin couldn't keep him, because he's a single man and hardly ever at home. So"—Chogyal shrugged—"with nowhere else to go, he came to us."

It was the first time that I'd heard Kyi Kyi's background, and I can't pretend, dear reader, that I was unaffected by the tale. I remembered how jealous I'd been of Kyi Kyi when he first arrived, how resentful of the affection Chogyal showered on him and the food he gave him. But I also recalled how subdued the dog had been, and the poor condition of his coat. If I'd known the full story, I too would have felt sorry for him.

"Seems like you've started an animal shelter," remarked His Holiness's driver. "How has Mousie-Tung taken to the new orphan?"

My whiskers twitched irritably. His Holiness's driver had always seemed a rough sort to me. Why did he insist on calling me by that dreadful name?

"Oh, I think she is still making up her mind about him." Chogyal glanced at me as he delivered his typically generous assessment.

"Making up her mind?" Walking over to the cabinet, the driver reached out to stroke me. "In that case, she is a very wise cat. Most of us judge others only on appearances."

"And as we all know"—Chogyal clicked his attaché case shut—"appearances can be very deceptive."

The next morning when I visited the assistants' office and saw Kyi Kyi in his basket, instead of ignoring him completely, I walked over and sniffed at him tentatively. Kyi Kyi reciprocated in kind, before cocking his head and taking a good, long look at me. Through this moment of communication we reached an understanding of sorts.

I did not, however, climb into his basket and let him lick my face.

I'm not that kind of cat. And this is not that kind of book. But I didn't envy Kyi Kyi anymore. Chogyal could walk him and feed him and whisper sweet nothings to him as much as he liked, and it wouldn't bother me a bit. I knew that behind this appearance was another reality. As I was discovering, even the most powerful first impressions could mask a very different truth.

I also discovered that I felt a lot happier not being jealous. Envy and resentment were demanding emotions that had disturbed my own peace of mind. For my sake, too, there was little point in being consumed by unhappy and irrational feelings.

It was less than six months later that a letter arrived for His Holiness on the impressive embossed stationery of the new Institute for Other Development established by Jack. After his visit to Jokhang, he had handed over management of his Self-Development company to a colleague and created a partner institute focusing on

Other Development. The idea was to encourage as many people as possible to give their time, money, and social networking skills to worthy causes. Jack's first instinct had been to nominate those worthy causes. But in the spirit of Other Development, he had decided to let others choose the organizations they wanted to support.

Within just a few months, over 10,000 people had signed up as supporters, and over $3 million had been raised for a wide variety of charities operating around the world. The huge surge of support, said Jack, was thrilling, humbling, and life-affirming. He'd never felt happier or more fulfilled in his life.

Would His Holiness consider attending the inaugural conference of the institute later in the year, perhaps with an address on the true causes of happiness?

As Tenzin read Jack's letter to Chogyal, there was unusual emotion in his voice. "Even though I've worked here for more than twenty years," he said, "I still get surprised. When people allow the well-being of *others* to become their motivation, the results are simply . . ."

"Immeasurable?" offered Chogyal.

"Yes. Precisely."

CHAPTER FIVE

Is it easy living as the anonymous companion to a global celebrity? Some people believe that the unknown companions of very famous individuals must feel constantly overlooked and undervalued, like the drab hens to glorious roosters. When the rooster gets all the attention with his lustrous plumage and magnificent dawn arpeggios, wouldn't it be understandable if the hen sometimes yearned for her own time in the spotlight, too?

In the case of this particular hen, no.

Within my own small world of Jokhang, I am already as well known as it's possible to be. At Café Franc I am venerated as a rinpoche! And while His Holiness may appear frequently on TV, he also has to go through life being photographed and having microphones thrust in his face morning, noon, and night. He must answer the relentless questions of journalists asking him to explain elementary Buddhism—much like a professor of applied physics being asked incessantly to recite the multiplication tables. That the Dalai Lama manages to do this with genuine warmth and a sense of humor reveals something not only about his personal qualities but also about the value of Buddhist practices—most notably, the perfection of patience!

The reason I'm so categorical—if you'll excuse the pun—about not wanting to be famous is that I've been on the receiving end of a great deal of media attention. This fact may surprise you. Why, you may wonder, have you not already come across the Dalai Lama's cat in the pages of *Vanity Fair*, photographed perhaps by the great Patrick Demarchelier? Or preening her whiskers and folding her long, gray boots with studied insouciance, having invited *Hello!* magazine to survey the delights of her sumptuous Himalayan boudoir? It pains me to admit that the media attention I received wasn't of the glossy magazine variety. Photographed? Yes. Celebrity pages? Alas, no.

It began one spring morning when His Holiness rose from his meditation an hour earlier than usual and got ready to venture outside. Changes to his routine were not unheard of—he often had trips to take or ceremonies to preside over. But that morning, even though his two executive assistants had reported early for duty, there was no sign of his driver. I realized His Holiness could not be going far. Hearing the sound of chanting across the courtyard, I also realized that he wouldn't be attending the usual morning proceedings at the temple. As the chief of protocol began checking security, parking, and other arrangements, it became clear we were expecting visitors. Who could they be?

Cars began arriving and dropping off journalists and TV crews from a variety of international media outlets. They were ushered along a path that led from behind the temple into the forested area nearby. Next came news that the car carrying His Holiness's visitor was approaching. His Holiness began making his way downstairs, followed by Tenzin and Chogyal, with Kyi Kyi on his leash trailing behind. Curious to discover what was happening, I tagged along.

As I did, I overheard snippets of information about the visitor: "Free Tibet campaign"; "Order of the British Empire." Her philanthropy was mentioned, as was the fact that she maintained a low-key lifestyle, dividing her time between homes in London and Scotland.

Just as the Dalai Lama appeared outside, his visitor arrived. An elegant lady with blonde, shoulder-length hair and vivacious features, she was clad not in the kind of conservative or formal clothing most of His Holiness's visitors wear but in a waxed outdoor jacket, khaki chinos, and brown hiking boots.

You know me quite well enough by now, dear reader, to realize that I never divulge the identity of His Holiness's visitors. Let's just say that this one was an absolutely fabulous English actress who has appeared in numerous television and stage productions and is a patron of several good causes.

After the traditional greeting, the Dalai Lama and his visitor began to walk toward the forest. I followed in their footsteps, while at a discreet distance behind me the rest of the entourage brought up the rear.

"I'm deeply grateful to you for lending your support to our cause," the actress said.

"The destruction of forests is a subject that should concern us all," replied the Dalai Lama. "I am glad to help."

The English lady spoke about the importance of forests as the "green lungs" of the planet, essential for converting carbon dioxide into oxygen. Forests are being dramatically reduced in size each day to make way for maize and palm-oil plantations, she pointed out, leading to soil erosion and pollution of vital water supplies, as well as loss of biodiversity. Many species, like the orangutan, are now threatened, she explained, because there are so few places left for them to live.

"Saving the forests is not only a question of money," she said. "There also has to be awareness and education. We need to motivate as many people as possible to take action, or at the very least, to support the idea of reforestation. Because you are so well known and so widely supported, your support will help us get the message across."

Taking her hand in his own, His Holiness said, "Together, we can combine our activities for the best result. You have been very, very generous in supporting so much of this work personally. And your support of the Free Tibet campaign and other charities has been exemplary."

She shrugged modestly. "I just feel it is the right thing to do."

By now we were walking along a path in the forest. On either side of us, the ground was carpeted in primrose and mistletoe. Large rhododendron bushes blossomed in extravagant displays of pink and red.

"If we allow ourselves to get too caught up in consumerism, we risk destroying all this," the actress said, gesturing around us.

His Holiness nodded in agreement. "You have very good motivation—giving without expecting to receive something back."

"Oh, I'm not concerned about that. I feel lucky to be able to give."

As the Dalai Lama chuckled, she regarded him inquiringly. "Don't you think so?"

"Very fortunate," His Holiness agreed. "But lucky? Perhaps not so much. In Buddhism, we follow the principle of karma, the law of cause and effect. There can be no effect, such as success, without a cause."

"I *have* worked at my career for many years," she conceded. "I've been through some pretty rough times."

"We would call things like hard work 'conditions,'" the Dalai Lama said, "not causes. Conditions are needed, certainly, for karma to germinate, just as a tree requires soil and moisture and heat to grow. But without a karmic cause, without that initial seed, it doesn't matter how favorable conditions are, there can be no effect."

The actress was following the Dalai Lama's words closely. The conversation had taken an unexpected turn, as it often does when His Holiness senses that someone would benefit from a particular insight.

"If hard work is only a condition, then what is the karmic cause for success?" she asked.

His Holiness gave her a look of immense benevolence. "Generosity," he answered. "The success you currently enjoy arises from your past generosity. And the generosity you are practicing now means that you will enjoy more success in the future."

We had been walking along the path for some minutes—farther than I had ever ventured on my own—when we came to a place where the forest suddenly stopped, giving way to a scarred moonscape of bald rock and sandy soil, with only a few, long-dead tree stumps left of what had once been lush vegetation.

His Holiness and the actress paused for a moment. Several holes had already been dug in preparation for a tree-planting ceremony. Pine saplings stood beside the holes, along with some wheelbarrows of soil. Journalists were assembled in readiness, cameras trained on the pair as they made their way out of the forest and across the wasteland.

As cameras whirred and members of the entourage closed in behind us, I felt a sudden need to attend to the call of nature. Being a cat of customarily high standards when it comes to such matters, I decided to look for a place that offered privacy and loose soil. A large banner bearing the logo of the actress's charity was stretched across the area where photos would be taken later. It seemed to provide the perfect screening.

Unnoticed, I ducked behind the banner. In the quietness back there, I discovered row upon row of fir saplings, just like the ones about to be ceremonially planted. Rising behind them was every cat's dream—a large mound of rich, loamy potting soil.

The very sight of it made me spring into action and scamper up the side with kittenish glee. I scattered soil this way and that as I clambered toward the summit, relishing my discovery. Once atop the mound, I sniffed at the earth, searching for a place of maximum comfort.

It was calm and quiet under the forest canopy as I sat meditatively. The early morning air—crisp, pine-scented—was bright with the mellifluous chorus of dawn birds. In the distance, I could hear a voice—the actress's?—making an announcement, followed by a smattering of applause.

And then it happened. The banner, and all my privacy, suddenly fell away. A moment of planned drama designed to reveal the full scale of the reforestation project instead was focused on me.

Don't get me wrong. We cats are not prudish. But nor do we like to make an exhibition of ourselves—especially not in front of the assembled world media.

For a moment the only sound was the clicking and whirring of cameras. Then a ripple of laughter passed through the gathering. His Holiness was one of the first to chuckle. Then the actress said something about the soil now being well fertilized.

My only concern, however, was to get away as fast as possible. I descended the earth mound even faster than I'd climbed it and scrambled into the undergrowth. Without pausing, I rushed back toward the temple and across the courtyard to the safety of home.

I had discovered a way of gaining access to the quarters I shared with the Dalai Lama that didn't involve waiting for anyone to open a door. Slipping into the ground-floor laundry, I hopped up onto a shelf and then walked along a ledge to a window that opened into the dining room. There, exhausted by the early morning exertions, I curled up in a large armchair and fell asleep.

I was awakened by the delicious aroma of grilled steak, prepared in the way that just one person could possibly cook it. Only when I lifted my head did I become aware that the dining room was now occupied. The Dalai Lama had returned to other duties, but he had left the actress and several members of the reforestation entourage in the care of Tenzin and Lobsang, the translator, and the translator's assistant. They were now sitting around the table eating a hearty breakfast of steak and eggs, while Mrs. Trinci fussed over them, offering extra servings of fried mushrooms, onion rings, and French toast. Seeing me stir, she soon returned with a small, white china dish on which she had thoughtfully arranged several bite-size portions of steak. She placed it on the floor beside me.

As we all attacked our breakfast with gusto, the conversation at the table moved from the tree-planting ceremony to the reforestation campaign and the actress's busy calendar for the rest of the year. Then, after a pause, she mused, "I had the most interesting conversation with His Holiness earlier about karma. It's not a subject we know much about in the West."

Tenzin had been following the actress ever since his days as a student at Oxford, and he relished the opportunity to talk to her. "Yes, that has always struck me as a little strange. The law of cause and effect is the assumed basis of all Western technology. Nothing is causeless; everything occurs as the result of something else. But as soon as one ventures beyond the immediate, material realm, Westerners talk about luck, fate, or divine intervention."

The group digested this in silence. "I suppose," continued Tenzin, "the difficulty is that karma is not instantly apparent. It can take time for causes to yield effects. Because of this, it may seem that there is no relationship between cause and effect."

"Yes," agreed the actress. "His Holiness was saying that whatever wealth or success one enjoys in the present moment arises from previous generosity, not from hard work, or taking risks, or pursuing opportunities that are *conditions* rather than causes."

"True," agreed Tenzin. "For karma to ripen, you need both—both the causes *and* the conditions."

"It's no secret among our little group here"—the actress gestured to her fellow campaigners—"that a curious thing happened the year I made a significant financial donation to the reforestation campaign."

There were knowing smiles around the table.

"I made the donation in May. Then, in December, I received exactly the same amount in a dividend I could never have foreseen. A lot of people said it was karma."

Everyone at the table laughed.

The actress turned to Tenzin. "Would that be the correct interpretation?"

"I can understand why people might think that," he replied. "But it's important not to be too literal. Because you give someone something one day doesn't mean you have created the cause to receive exactly the same thing another day. Karma operates not so much as some external credit-and-debit ledger but more as an energy, a charge that grows over time. This is how even small acts of generosity, especially when motivated by the best intention, can become causes for much greater wealth in the future."

The actress and her colleagues were studying him closely.

"Where it gets interesting," Tenzin continued, "is that in giving, we not only create the causes for future wealth, we also create the conditions for the ripening of whatever wealth karma we already possess. Hard work and shrewd business dealings are conditions for wealth but so too is generosity."

"There's logic to what you say," said the actress. "And it interests me that Jesus also said, 'As you sow, so shall you reap.'"

"The notion of karma was widely accepted in the earliest days of Christianity," agreed Tenzin. "Not only were important symbols imported from the East, such as the sign of the fish and the halo"—he gestured to a wall hanging of Buddha crowned by a brilliant azure halo—"but it seems to me that the central teachings of loving thy neighbor, having compassion, and the like may also have made their way along the Old Silk Road two thousand years ago."

The looks of concentration on the visitors' faces were keen.

"One thing I don't understand about karma," the actress said, "is where it all happens. If there is no God deciding to punish or reward, and no cosmic computer keeping a record, where is it all happening?"

"That question goes to the heart of it," replied Tenzin. "It is all happening in the continuum of our minds. Our experience of reality is a lot more subjective than we generally realize. We are not simply passive receptors of events. At all times we are actively projecting our own personal version of reality onto the world around us. Two people in the same circumstances will have very different experiences of what happened. This is because they have different karma.

"The law of cause and effect," Tenzin continued, "says that, step by step, we can create the causes to experience reality in a way that results in greater contentment and abundance, and we can avoid the causes of unhappiness and lack of resources. Buddha himself summed it up best when he said: 'The thought manifests as the word; the word manifests as the deed; the deed develops into habit; and habit hardens into character. So watch the thought and its ways with care, and let it spring from love born out of concern for all beings . . . As the shadow follows the body, as we think, so we become.'"

A short while later, the actress and her party rose from the table, thanking Tenzin and the others for all their help. They were gathering their jackets and scarves when the actress looked over at the armchair on which I was seated, legs tucked neatly under my body.

"Good heavens! Is that the cat . . . you know . . . from this morning?"

Tenzin glanced over at me with the same poker face he had worn on the afternoon he had discovered me seated on the lotus cushion at Café Franc.

"She looks similar," he conceded.

"I've never seen Snow Lion venture so far away," said Lobsang.

"Himalayan cats are quite popular here," ventured Lobsang's assistant.

The actress shook her head with a wry smile. "Well, it certainly was an unexpected performance."

Late that afternoon, Tenzin was briefing the Dalai Lama on the day's events as the two of them enjoyed their green tea, accompanied on this occasion by wafer-thin biscotti baked by the ever-bountiful Mrs. Trinci. Having discussed most of the day's activities, His Holiness turned to the tree-planting ceremony.

"How did the breakfast go? I hope the visitors were happy with the outcome."

"It went very well, Your Holiness. And our guest phoned me just a short while ago to say how thrilled she is with the awareness being created."

"There were a lot of media crews this morning," observed the Dalai Lama. "I have never seen so many television cameras at Jokhang!"

"The event was well covered by the media," said Tenzin. "But the real booster is a YouTube video that instantly went viral. Apparently, it already has more than ten million hits."

"For a tree-planting ceremony?" His Holiness raised his eyebrows.

"It begins with that. But the real star of the show"—Tenzin turned to look in my direction—"is our little Rinpoche."

The Dalai Lama burst out laughing. Then, making an effort to contain himself, he said, "Perhaps we should not laugh. I am not sure who got more of a surprise, our Rinpoche or the journalists."

Coming over to where I was sitting, he scooped me up in his arms and stroked me slowly. "This morning when we all woke up, none of us guessed you were about to become—how do you say?—an international sensation. But you have created more awareness of the problem facing forests in a single morning than some people create in a whole lifetime."

I began to purr.

"Most interesting karma."

CHAPTER SIX

Fur balls. There are few things more unpleasant, don't you agree, dear reader?

Oh, come, come. There's no need to play the innocent with me! Just because you're human doesn't make you immune to self-obsession. Is it not the case that from time to time you experience excessive concern about how you come across to other beings? That you obsess about your clothing, footwear, adornments, and grooming, all of which have rather more to do with an image you wish to project to the world than matters of simple practicality?

When talking about yourself, that subtle aside about the fancy brand of merchandise recently acquired, the romantic attention you are receiving, or the extraordinary yoga position you are now capable of assuming—is it not the case that such remarks are also intended to conjure up a particular impression you wish to create about yourself?

And who, pray tell, occupies the majority of your thoughts from the moment you wake up till the time you go to sleep? Who, exactly, is the cause of your greatest anxiety and stress? Can you think of a certain party—perhaps not so far from the space you currently occupy—who at some time has become so caught up in a downward spiral of self-obsession that despite all their frenetic licking, scratching, and grooming, despite all their crazed efforts to feel better about themselves, all they have succeeded in doing is ingesting such large quantities of self-regarding detritus that they have made themselves sick—quite literally, perhaps?

If an uncomfortable lump is forming in your throat simply from reading these few paragraphs, then you most certainly understand the vexation of fur balls. If not, you are clearly a better adjusted being than most, in which case I apologize for impugning your character. You certainly have no need to read this chapter, so may I suggest you proceed immediately to the next?

Having been torn away from my mother and family at an early age, there are certain aspects of cat behavior of which I was wholly ignorant. Which was why my first fur-ball experience was as unexpected as it was unpleasant. One of the burdens of being a sumptuously beautiful cat of the kind that occasionally graces the boxes of the most expensive Belgian pralines is that grooming can become a compulsive activity. It's all too easy to get caught up in a cycle of licking and preening without realizing what the consequences will be.

The morning I spent on the filing cabinet, vigorously engaged in just this activity, Tenzin glanced sharply in my direction several times, and Chogyal even came over and tried to distract me—to no avail. The initial tingle I had felt seemed to grow more and more intense and widespread until I couldn't stop licking!

And then it struck. Suddenly, I knew I had to get down onto the floor. Making my way across the office, directly past Kyi Kyi's basket, I had no sooner reached the corridor when I felt my stomach turn. It was as though all my insides wanted to come out. I crouched low on the carpet, my whole body racked with wheezing. The rhythm of the violent spasms increased rapidly until . . . well, it's probably best that I spare you the details.

Leaping to his feet, Chogyal seized a copy of that day's newspaper. He used the women's fashion section to clean up the rug on which I had deposited copious quantities of my own fur. I slunk to the kitchen for a cleansing drink, and by the time I made my way back, there was no sign of the horror that had befallen me in the calm sanctuary of the hallway.

I resumed my place on the filing cabinet, falling into a deep slumber. There's nothing like a good, long sleep to allow unpleasantness to recede into the past.

Except that on that occasion, I was awoken by a powerful and disorientating fragrance. Was that not the unmistakable aroma of Kouros, which usually preceded Franc by several yards? But I wasn't at Café Franc!

Moments later came confirmation in the form of Franc's unmistakably San Franciscan cadences.

Neither Chogyal nor Tenzin was in the office, but there, in the door frame, was the round-eared silhouette of Marcel. Moments later, Chogyal arrived with a leash. Stirring Kyi Kyi from his slumbers, he clipped the leash to his collar and led him to where Marcel was straining at his own lead, tail wagging in a frenzy of anticipation.

Franc and Chogyal talked in the corridor, while the two dogs commenced sniffing each other's backsides. Completely absorbed in what was happening, Franc didn't notice me on my viewing platform, watching events unfold. Although I had been disconcerted by the unexpected arrival of Tenzin in Café Franc some weeks earlier, as I watched events unfold now, it all began to make a kind of sense.

Franc was on his best behavior. Formally dressed in a dark jacket and polished brogues, he was as solicitous as when the most important of VIPs appeared in his café. Chogyal, meantime, was his usual unaffected self, as he related the story of how Kyi Kyi had come to take up residence at Jokhang.

The men took the dogs for a walk in the courtyard outside. Crossing to a window that afforded a better view, I continued to watch the proceedings. Free of their leashes, Marcel and Kyi Kyi chased each other, playing and scuffling. It seemed that the two dogs could indeed become friends.

On their return, Chogyal and Franc began discussing Kyi Kyi's eating and sleeping habits. Then I heard Chogyal saying, "All of us, including His Holiness, would be very grateful if you would consider—"

"No need to consider," Franc assured him. "The two dogs are going to get on fine. It will be my honor."

Chogyal looked down at Kyi Kyi with a smile. "He has been here only a short time, but we will miss him."

"I can bring him back to visit," Franc replied.

At that moment the door to His Holiness's office opened and out he came.

As Franc bowed with elaborate formality, the Dalai Lama, chuckling, brought his hands to his forehead.

"This is Franc, Your Holiness. He has kindly agreed to look after Kyi Kyi."

"Very good." The Dalai Lama reached out to take Franc's hand between his own. "Wonderful compassion." Then he spotted all the blessing strings tied around Franc's wrist. "You have received many blessings?"

As usual, Franc recited the list of initiations he had received from various high-ranking lamas during the preceding decade. His Holiness listened patiently before asking, "Who is your teacher?"

"All of the lamas who have given me initiations," replied Franc, as though repeating an article of faith.

"It is useful," said His Holiness, "to have a regular teacher and attend classes. Initiations and textbooks are helpful. More helpful is to practice under the guidance of a qualified teacher. If you wanted to learn the piano, would you not find the best piano teacher you could— and stick with him or her? It is the same with the Dharma. Like that."

The advice seemed revelatory to Franc, who took a while to process it. After a few moments he asked, "Is there any teacher you'd recommend?"

"For you?" His Holiness seemed captivated by the gold Om dangling from Franc's left ear as he considered an answer. Finally, he said, "You may ask Geshe Wang-po, here at Namgyal Monastery. I think he would be right for you."

A short while later, Franc left Jokhang, taking Kyi Kyi with him. I was curious to know how the day's events would be recounted under the jaunty umbrellas of Café Franc. And I couldn't help wondering if I would retain my position of grace and favor at the café, between the latest issues of *Vogue* and *Vanity Fair*. Now that Franc had accepted guardianship of a being who was sure to become known as the Dalai Lama's Dog, would I still be the main object of such veneration?

I also wondered why, at odd times over the next few days, Chogyal and Tenzin would glance at each other, mutter "Geshe Wangpo," and snort with laughter.

The answers to all these questions soon became apparent. Beginning with Geshe Wangpo. It just so happened that I was resting on my favorite windowsill a week or so later, when once again, I was awakened by the familiar scent of Franc's aftershave. Although distant, it nevertheless curled like a ribbon through the air, from the courtyard below to where I lay in the pose of the up-turned lizard. Opening my eyes, I spotted Franc walking from the gates of Jokhang toward the temple.

Curiosity getting the better of me, I was soon on my way downstairs, manifesting on the steps of the temple as Franc approached, where I performed a deep and luxuriant sun salutation as though I had spent the whole morning idling there. Franc seemed reassured by my familiar presence on this important visit and bent to stroke me.

It was only a short while later that Geshe Wangpo emerged from the temple. About 50 years old, short, round-faced, and stocky, he emanated an authority well beyond his stature, as though his physical appearance barely hinted at an extraordinary, even wrathful, power. The moment he appeared, I realized why Chogyal and Tenzin had been so amused when the Dalai Lama had recommended Geshe Wangpo as a teacher for Franc: a more heavy-duty lama would be hard to imagine.

Still, he smiled when Franc introduced himself.

"I wonder if you would consider taking me on as a student?" asked Franc, the cloud of Kouros, the golden Om, and the tight black clothing seeming even more out of place at that particular moment.

"You can attend my classes on Tuesday nights," said Geshe Wangpo. "It is important to make sure of someone before accepting them as your teacher."

"The Dalai Lama himself recommended you," countered Franc.

"Even so, maybe you do not like my approach. We all have different styles, different temperaments." It seemed almost as if Geshe Wangpo was trying to dissuade him. "Perhaps it is wise to take your time before deciding. Once you accept someone as your adviser"—he wagged a finger—"you must be willing to follow the advice."

But Franc was not to be deterred. "If His Holiness suggested you"—his tone was reverential—"that's good enough for me."

"Okay, okay," agreed the lama. Nodding toward his new student's wrist, he added, "You already have many initiations. Your commitments must keep you very busy."

"Commitments?"

"The ones you made when you received your initiations."

"I did?"

Geshe Wangpo's brow furrowed. "Why seek initiations into a practice if you don't want to follow the practice?"

"I didn't realize . . . " For the first time ever, Franc actually looked sheepish.

"Which empowerments have you received?"

Franc began his familiar roll call of dates, lamas, and esoteric initiations—only this time, he repeated it in a most unfamiliar tone. It was as though the recitation of each successive initiation, rather than a show of braggadocio, was an admission of ignorance and neglect.

When he had finally finished, Geshe Wangpo regarded him sternly before bursting into laughter.

"What?" Franc asked, all too aware that he was the object of the lama's amusement.

"You Westerners!" Geshe Wangpo managed after a while. "Too funny!"

"I don't understand." Franc hunched his shoulders.

"The Dharma is an inner journey," Geshe Wangpo said, touching his heart. "Not about saying you are Buddhist, or wearing clothes to show you are Buddhist, or even believing you are Buddhist. What is 'Buddhist'?" He gestured with open hands. "Just a word. Just a label. What is the value of a label if the product inside isn't authentic? Like a fake Rolex." He delivered a mischievous glance.

Franc shuffled uneasily.

Geshe Wangpo wagged his finger from side to side. "We don't want fake Rolexes here at Namgyal Monastery," he said. "Only the real deal."

"What should I do about my blessing strings?" Franc asked unhappily.

"Your choice," Geshe Wangpo told him. "Only you can know about such things—it is not for someone else to say." Then, regarding his new student's pensive features, he tugged Franc by the arm. "Come. Let's walk around the temple. I need to stretch my legs."

The two men set off, circumambulating the temple in a clockwise fashion. I followed closely behind. Geshe Wangpo asked Franc where he was from, and Franc began telling him about his upbringing in California, his passion for travel, the journey that had brought him all the way to Dharamsala, and his entirely unexpected decision to open Café Franc.

"I've always felt this tug toward Buddhism," Franc told the lama. "I thought that taking initiations and receiving empowerments from high lamas was what I should do. I knew I should meditate, too, but I have a busy life. I didn't realize that I needed a teacher or should be going to regular classes."

Geshe Wangpo reached out and squeezed Franc's hand briefly after this confession. "Let's make this your fresh start," he suggested. "Do you know the Four Noble Truths?"

Franc was hesitant. "I've heard them mentioned."

"The first teachings Buddha gave after he became enlightened were the Four Noble Truths. They are a very good place to begin an understanding. You see, Buddha is just like a doctor you go to see when you are feeling unwell. First, the doctor checks the symptoms. Then, he diagnoses the condition. Next, he says if it's possible to deal with the problem—makes a prognosis. Last, he prescribes the treatment. Buddha took exactly the same four steps when looking at our experience of life."

Franc was following the lama intently. "What symptoms did he find?"

"In general," said Geshe Wangpo, "a high level of dissatisfaction, or *dukkha* in Sanskrit. Dukkha means everything from trivial discomfort to the deepest physical and emotional suffering. Buddha understood that much of our experience of ordinary life is difficult. Stressful. It's hard to be us."

Franc was nodding in agreement.

"The causes of this dissatisfaction are many. The fact that we are born means we must face death and most probably the hardships of sickness and old age. Impermanence can be another cause of unhappiness. We can get things just the way we want them, and then"—the lama snapped his fingers—"change."

Geshe Wangpo continued. "But the underlying reason for our dissatisfaction, the root cause, is that we mistake the way that things exist. We see objects and people as separate and independent from us. We believe them to have characteristics, qualities, that we are attracted to or repelled by. We think everything is happening outside us and we are just reacting to it—as though it's all coming at us from the outside."

They walked for several steps in silence before Franc asked, "Why is it a mistake to see it that way?"

"Because when we look very hard, we can't find an essence to any person or object, including me. We can't find any qualities that exist separate from our own minds."

"You're saying"—Franc spoke faster than usual—"that there's nothing out there and we're making it all up?"

"No. But that is the most common misunderstanding. This subtle truth is called 'dependent arising,' and it can take much study and meditation to understand. But it's the most amazingly powerful concept—life-changing when we begin to comprehend it. Just as quantum scientists have confirmed, what Buddha taught is that *the way* things exist, *how* things exist, depends, in part, on our own minds. This means that the Third Noble Truth, the prognosis, is a positive one."

"Because we can work on our minds?" ventured Franc.

"Yes, yes!" Geshe Wangpo nodded briskly. "If all this dissatisfaction, all this dukkha, were coming from out there, it would be impossible to do much about it. But because it originates in the mind itself, well, we have some hope. So the Fourth Noble Truth is the treatment—what we can do about our mental problems." Again he regarded Franc with a daring smile.

But Franc was too absorbed in what the lama was saying to take offense. "So what's the treatment?" he wanted to know.

"All of Buddha's teachings," Geshe Wangpo replied. "He is said to have given eighty-four thousand of them."

"The Dharma?"

"Yes. Do you know what *Dharma* means?"

Franc shrugged. "Buddha's philosophy?"

Geshe Wangpo tilted his head, "Broadly speaking, you could say that. In Buddhism we also interpret Dharma to mean 'cessation,' as in the end of dissatisfaction, the end of dukkha. This is the purpose of Buddha's teachings."

The lama paused for a moment as they reached a point behind the temple where a large tree formed an umbrella over the pathway. The ground beside them was scattered with leaves.

"You know, Buddha was once asked a mysterious question about the universe. The way he answered the question is very interesting." Geshe Wangpo bent down to scoop up a handful of leaves. "He asked his students, 'Are there more leaves in my hand, or on the floor of the forest all around us?' The students said, 'On the floor of the forest.' So Buddha replied, 'The leaves in my hand represent the knowledge that leads to the end of suffering.' In this way"—Geshe Wangpo opened his hand, letting the leaves flutter to the ground—"Buddha was very clear about the purpose of his teachings."

"If there are eighty-four thousand of them, where do you begin?" asked Franc as they continued the circumambulation.

"The Lam Rim, or graduated path to enlightenment, is a good place to start," the lama told him. "It teaches us to become more aware of our own mental behavior, to replace negative patterns of thought with more positive ones."

"Sounds like psychotherapy."

"Exactly! Lama Yeshe, one of the first lamas to bring Tibetan Buddhism to the West, used to say exactly that: 'Be your own therapist.' He wrote a book with that title."

The two of them continued in silence for a while before Franc asked, "Is it true that some lamas are clairvoyant?"

Geshe Wangpo glanced at him sharply. "Why do you ask?"

"I'm just wondering . . . what negative patterns of thought I might need to work on."

"You don't need to be clairvoyant to know that." The lama's voice was firm.

"No?"

"Everyone has the same basic problem. Expressed in different ways. Our main problem is that we are all 'I' specialists."

Franc was uncomprehending. "But I don't know anything about vision."

"Not that kind of eye. I as in 'me, myself, and I.'"

"Oh! Uh-huh."

"We don't stop thinking about ourselves the whole time. Even when this makes us unhappy and uptight. If we focus too much on ourselves, we make ourselves sick. We have this constant inner chatter going morning, noon, and night, this inner monologue. But paradoxically, the more we are able to think about making other beings happy, the happier we become ourselves."

Franc looked despondent as he absorbed this. "Not much hope for people like me, is there?"

"Why?"

"I have a very busy restaurant. I'm in there every day of the week and work long hours. I just don't have time to think about making other beings happy."

"But I would say you have a great advantage!" Geshe Wangpo retorted. "The happiness of others isn't an abstract idea. You don't have to go to the mountains to meditate on it. You begin at home and at work, with the people and other beings in your life. If you have customers, think of every one of them as an opportunity to practice loving kindness. You can serve them a coffee, or you can serve them a coffee and a smile—something that makes them happier for the moment they are with you. If you have a staff—well, you are a very important person in their lives. You have great power to make them happy—or miserable."

"I didn't realize," said Franc, "that running a business and making money could be part of being a Buddhist."

"Of course! Everything is part of the Dharma. Your business. Your family. Everything. When you first start, Dharma practice is like a trickle of water high on a mountain. The trickle affects just a small, green area an inch or two wide, as the water flows along the ground. But as you practice Dharma more and more, the flow gets stronger and is joined by other streams. It may occasionally falter, like a waterfall, or disappear beneath the surface, but it keeps going, gathering strength. Eventually, it becomes like a very large river that's broad and powerful and the center of everything in your life.

"Think about your Dharma practice like that—every day growing more and more. Giving more and more happiness to others—and gaining more and more happiness yourself."

Several days later I was sitting on the filing cabinet in the executive assistants' office when I felt a familiar tingling—a powerful compulsion to lick. I began grooming, though even as I did, I remembered the horror of the fur ball experience and the words of Geshe Wangpo: "If we focus too much on ourselves, we make ourselves sick." I also recalled the lama's advice about focusing more on others. After some moments, I forced myself to stop and instead hopped down off the filing cabinet.

Tenzin had his spectacles on and was absorbed in an important e-mail from the Dalai Lama to the British prime minister. Chogyal was finalizing the itinerary for His Holiness's forthcoming visit to Southeast Asia.

With a soft meow I padded over to Chogyal and nudged his hand from the keyboard.

The two executive assistants exchanged glances. As Chogyal hesitated, I gave the back of his hand an appreciative lick.

"What's this, my little Snow Lion?" he asked, surprised by my display of affection.

"Most unusual," remarked Tenzin, before adding, "She was licking again. Did you notice? Perhaps she is molting."

"I didn't notice." Chogyal stretched to open his desk drawer. "But I may be able to help."

From his drawer he produced a bag containing a comb and brush. Then, lifting me off his desk, he took me out to the hallway, where he began combing through my thick coat, removing large tufts of fur with every sweep.

I began purring with contentment. And the purring continued for the next ten minutes as he combed my back, then each side, then my white and luxuriantly fluffy tummy. Chogyal removed every tangle, until my fur shimmered with silkiness. I had rarely felt such bliss. Head back and eyes shut, I thought that if this were the reward one got for wishing to make other beings happy, I should certainly be doing more of it!

In the weeks after Franc's adoption of Kyi Kyi and his first meeting with Geshe Wangpo, I paid special attention to the status quo at Café Franc. Marcel and Kyi Kyi were now a confirmed double act, the two dogs sharing a basket under the counter and being taken for walks together. Gone was Kyi Kyi's lank hair and scrawny appearance, replaced by bright-eyed mischief.

I was relieved that there was no perceptible change in behavior toward me. I was still Rinpoche, the Dalai Lama's Cat, occupying the best shelf in the house and fed the tastiest morsels from each day's *plat du jour.*

But the change in Franc was impossible to miss. The very first time I saw him after we circumambulated the temple, I noticed immediately that the gold Om was gone from his ear. Looking down at his wrist, I saw that he had also removed the blessing strings. Obviously he had taken to heart Geshe Wangpo's pointed references to fake Rolexes and decided that the authentic version, though much more difficult to acquire, was preferable.

Every morning Franc would arrive at work half an hour later than in the past, following an early morning meditation session. He also took to wearing a baseball cap that stayed on his head throughout the day and into the evening. At first I couldn't work out what was going on with the cap. But once, when he removed it briefly to scratch his head, I noticed a layer of fuzz. As his hair grew longer, the caricature of his former self began to fade. There were fewer references to Buddhist this and Dharma that. He rarely pointed out that I was the Dalai Lama's cat and didn't once mention the origin of Kyi Kyi, the newest member of the Café Franc household.

In the curious way that karma works, Franc's metamorphosis couldn't have been better timed.

One day at noon, an earnest-looking couple arrived at the café and worked their way through the luncheon menu. Dressed in modest taupe colors and ascetic in appearance, they seemed like just another pair of Western intellectuals doing their India tour. Perhaps he was a lecturer in Pali Buddhist Studies from some American campus. Perhaps she taught Ashtanga yoga or was a vegan chef at an alternative health center. From the way they chewed their food mindfully, they seemed to be treating the Café Franc experience very seriously.

It was only an hour and a half later, when their dessert plates had been cleared and their coffee cups were almost empty, that the male of the pair summoned Franc with a surprisingly assertive jab of his right index finger. This wasn't the first time the two men had spoken. He had already grilled Franc extensively before choosing his main course, an experience Franc had managed with newfound graciousness.

"Just thought I would properly introduce myself," he said in cultivated New England tones. "Charles Hayder of *Hayder's Food Guides*."

To say that Franc was surprised would be an understatement. He was astonished! *Hayder's Food Guides* were among the most revered on the planet. Widely published and highly regarded, they could make or break a dining establishment.

Franc blurted out something about it being an honor.

"I heard about Café Franc from a friend in New Delhi. We thought we'd give you a try," Hayder said, nodding toward his wife, who smiled brightly. "I have to say, the meal we've had today was outstanding. Every element of it! I'd go so far as to call it the best in the region. We'll be providing a commendation in our India feature for *The New York Times*."

Franc was so overcome that for the first time in his life, he seemed at a loss for words.

"Only one disappointment," continued Hayder, more confidentially. "I was told the maitre d' was the most appalling Buddhist wannabe. Was I misinformed?"

Franc paused for a moment, looking down at his naked wrist. "No. No, you weren't," he said. "He was."

"Ah, so a facelift at Café Franc?"

"It goes deeper than that," suggested Franc.

"Of course it does!" chimed Hayder. "Permeates the whole experience." He allowed himself a wry smile. "As much as it goes against the grain, I'm going to have to write an entirely favorable review."

It would be foolish, dear reader, to imagine that a single teaching from a high lama would result in a permanent cure for self-cherishing in either cats or humans. Of all the delusions, self-obsession is perhaps the wiliest at disguising itself, seeming to disappear from view completely, only to be revealed in monstrous dimensions in a transmuted form.

I hadn't coughed up my last fur ball.

Nor had Franc.

But a change had occurred. A new direction was being pursued. And in the months ahead, there were to be all kinds of intriguing developments at Café Franc, as I was to discover.

CHAPTER SEVEN

Are you a creature of habit? Among the coffee mugs in your kitchen, is there a favorite that you prefer, even though any of them would serve the purpose? Have you developed personal rituals—perhaps in the way you read a newspaper, enjoy a glass of wine an evening, or conduct your ablutions—that provide a reassuring sense that life is as it should be?

If your answer to any of these probing questions is yes, then, dear reader, you may very well have been a cat in a previous lifetime. And I, for one, can think of no higher distinction!

We cats are the most habitual of creatures. Preferred sun loungers, meal times, hidey holes, and scratching posts are among the considerations in which we take daily satisfaction. And it is exactly because many humans embrace routine that we even consider allowing them to share our homes, let alone retain them as members of our staff.

There are, of course, some disruptions that we all enjoy. How dull life would be without, for example, the occasional sampling of a new delicacy, like the day that Mrs. Trinci arrived at Jokhang triumphantly bearing a tray of roasted-eggplant lasagna for all to taste. Or the morning's entertainment at Café Franc, when an Asian gentleman laboriously broke his breakfast toast into small pieces, applied butter and marmalade to each individually, then used chopsticks to eat them.

Such incidents are a welcome diversion. But when more important events threaten the comfortable pattern of life, that's a different matter entirely. I am talking here about change. A favorite Dalai Lama theme. The only constant in life, as Buddha himself said.

Speaking for most cats and humans, it's probably accurate to say that change is something we would rather have happen to beings other than ourselves. But, alas, there seems to be no escaping it. There you are, assuming that your familiar life, with all its reassuring rituals and habits, is set to continue indefinitely. Then, out of nowhere, like a slavering, unleashed pit bull or some such demonic archetype appearing suddenly on the pavement before you, everything is thrown into wild disarray.

My own discovery of this truth began uneventfully enough one morning when I strolled unsuspectingly from my morning meditation with His Holiness into the executive assistants' office. Nothing was said initially. That particular working day began like any other, with the usual buzz of phone calls and meetings and the driver arriving to take His Holiness to the airport. I knew he would be away for two weeks, visiting seven countries in Europe. Having lived at Jokhang for more than eight months, during which His Holiness had made frequent trips abroad, I was used to the idea that he had to travel often. When he went away, his staff would make sure I was well cared for.

Usually.

On this occasion, however, things turned out very differently. Midway through that first morning, two men in paint-spattered overalls arrived in the office. Chogyal took them through to the quarters I shared with His Holiness, where they were soon setting up ladders and covering the floor with plastic sheeting.

Horrifying disfigurement rapidly followed. Photographs and thangkas were removed from walls, curtains stripped from windows, furniture draped with canvas. Within minutes my rarefied sanctuary was reduced to unrecognizable chaos.

Chogyal picked me up, I thought for reassurance. I fully expected him to apologize for the upheaval, tell me that the painters would be finished in no time, and confirm that my home would soon be my own again. But events became only more distressing.

Carrying me back to his office, he placed me inside a hideous wooden box that had appeared on his desk. Made of rough-hewn wood, it was so small I could barely turn around inside. Before I could even protest, he was fastening the metal-grill lid and carrying the whole thing downstairs.

I didn't know which I felt more intensely—outrage or terror.

Outrage predominated to begin with. This was kid-nap! How dare he take such liberties! Had he forgotten who I was?! *And* the moment the Dalai Lama's back was turned! Of all people, the usually warmhearted Chog-yal! Whose malevolent influence had he fallen under? If His Holiness knew what was happening, I had no doubt he would have put an immediate end to it.

Chogyal walked through a section of Namgyal Mon-astery with which I was familiar before continuing on a path that I'd never traversed. As he walked, he chanted mantras under his breath in his usual, easygoing way, as though nothing untoward was happening. From time to time he paused for a brief conversation, on several occa-sions holding the cage so that others could look at me like some zoological exhibit. Glaring furiously through a crack between two pieces of wood, I caught glimpses only of red robes and sandaled feet. Had I been able to lash out and administer a severe claw-lashing, I most certainly would have.

Chogyal continued walking. And all of a sudden it occurred to me that this had happened before. Not to me personally—at least not in this particular lifetime. But there was a time in history when refined individu-als of higher breeding were wrenched from their homes and carted off to a bleak future. As students of European history will already have guessed, I'm referring to the French Revolution.

Had that been any different from what was hap-pening to me now? Had the mild-mannered Chogyal transmogrified into a sinister Tibetan Robespierre? Was the way he displayed me to those we met not precisely what had happened when the hapless aristocrats were wheeled through the streets of Paris to meet their grisly fate at the guillotine—a gruesome ritual I'd heard about while Tenzin munched on his lunchtime sandwich only the week before.

Suddenly I became afraid, more fearful with every step that Chogyal took into unknown territory. There might be no guillotine at the end of this particular journey, but for the first time I wondered, what if this were not a mistake? What if some plan had been agreed to with the Dalai Lama's consent? Perhaps His Holiness had made some oblique remark his assistants had interpreted to mean that he'd rather not have me around anymore. What if I was to be demoted from His Holiness's Cat to plain McLeod Ganj House Cat?

The area we were in now was rundown. Through the crack in the wood, I observed dirt pavements and barren gardens, pungent odors and the cries of children. Chogyal turned off the road and proceeded along a dirt path to an ugly concrete building. As he continued, I could just make out that we were in an open corridor with doors leading off both sides. Some of the doors were ajar, revealing rooms in which whole families were gathered, sitting on the floor around plates of food.

My captor fished a key out of his robe and unlocked a door, then stepped into a room and deposited the cage on the floor.

"Home sweet home," he said cheerfully, unlocking the metal grill, lifting me out, and placing my small, quaking form on what was evidently his duvet. "You'll have to stay with me, HHC, till the painters are finished," he explained, stroking me in a way that suggested that instead of putting me through the most harrowing ordeal of my life, he had merely taken a 20-minute walk. "It shouldn't be more than a week."

A whole week!

"They're repainting everything, walls, ceilings, window frames, and doors. By the time they're finished, it will feel like new. In the meantime, you can have a holiday with me. And my niece, Lasya, will take care of you."

A girl of about ten, with sharp eyes and dirty fingers, appeared from outside and knelt on the floor, where she began squealing at me in a high-pitched voice as though I were both stupid and hard of hearing.

Slinking to the top of the bed, ears flat back and tail limp, I crawled under the duvet. At least the smell of Chogyal on the bedclothes was familiar.

I took refuge in the darkness.

There I stayed for the next three days, sleeping away as many hours as I could. I emerged only to attend to the most urgent calls of nature, before returning to curl up in a miserable, fluffy ball.

Chogyal was away most of each day at work, and Lasya soon tired of trying to play with a cat who wouldn't respond. Her visits became infrequent and brief. Gradually, the sounds of families going about their day and the cooking aromas became more familiar. After three days of semi-wakefulness in the semi-darkness I came to a recognition: I was bored.

So, on day four, when Lasya arrived late in the afternoon, I crawled out from under the duvet and hopped onto the floor for the first time. There we discovered a new game, quite by accident. As I brushed up against her right foot, her big toe slipped inside my left ear, the other toes remaining on the outside. Wiggling her toes, she improvised a delightful ear massage—I found myself purring gratefully. Neither the Dalai Lama nor any of his staff were in the habit of putting their big toes in my ear, but as I discovered now, the sensation was utterly delightful. Left ear was soon followed by right, and as I looked up into Lasya's giggling face, I understood for the first time that my happiness didn't depend on being in particular surroundings.

I made my way to the door, and into the corridor. With Lasya as my minder, I padded tentatively toward the back of the building. In the very next room a woman and three children sat on the floor, stirring a pot on a single burner and chanting some sort of nursery rhyme. Having listened to them for the past three days as they prepared a variety of meals, I was curious to finally see them. Unlike the clamorous demons of my imagination, they seemed smaller somehow and more ordinary.

The moment I appeared, they stopped what they were doing and turned to stare. No doubt news of my arrival had passed down the corridor. Were they somehow overawed at finding themselves in the presence of the Dalai Lama's Cat? I felt sure they must be!

Eventually, one of the children, perhaps eight years old, made a move. Extracting a sliver of tender meat from the cooking pot, he blew on it to cool it before coming to offer it to me. I sniffed hesitantly. Café Franc's filet mignon this was not. But I was hungry. It smelled strangely appetizing. And as I took the meat from his hand and chewed it contemplatively, I had to admit it packed a tasty punch.

Continuing on our way, Lasya and I headed across the backyard—a desolate stretch of bare earth—to a wall about three feet high. When I jumped on top of the wall, I was surprised to find myself looking across an open area to a soccer pitch in the distance. Two teams of teenagers were battling in the dust for possession of a ball fashioned out of scrunched-up plastic bags bound tightly together with twine. *Now* I understood where all the shouting and excitement I had heard under the duvet was coming from.

Lasya perched beside me to watch the match, her legs dangling over the wall. She seemed to know the players and occasionally cried out encouragement. Settling next to her, I watched the game unfold: it was my first soccer match, and compared to the sedentary pace of life at Jokhang, it was riveting.

I scarcely noticed that dusk was falling, until I looked up and saw candles and lamps being lit in the homes all around us. The aromas of a dozen meals wafted on the evening breeze, along with sounds of clinking dishes, laughter and squabbling, running water and TV. How very different all this was from the sights and sounds of my favorite perch in the window of His Holiness's room. But I couldn't deny there was a vibrant energy to this place where all of life was lived out in the open.

The sun slid below the horizon, and the sky grew darker. Lasya had long since wandered back to her family, leaving me perched on the wall, my paws tucked neatly underneath me.

This was when I became aware of a movement at the side of the building, a fluid shadow slipping effortlessly down the side of a 40-gallon drum. A cat! And not just any cat but one who was unusually big and muscular, with dark stripes vividly defined. I had no doubt at all he was the same magnificent tiger tabby I had first seen across the temple courtyard, by the green light of the market stall. How long he had been sitting on the drum watching me, I couldn't guess. But his actions left me in no doubt about his interest.

Padding directly across the barren backyard from one side to the other, he ignored me completely, as if I didn't exist. Could he have *been* more obvious?

Suddenly I was all a-flutter. To anyone looking on, I might appear to be a cat sitting placidly on a wall. But my thoughts and emotions were in thrilling turmoil. The proprietorial way the tabby had strolled across the yard made it clear that this was his domain. Having ventured as far away as Jokhang, he was evidently a cat of some standing. Sure, the mackerel tabby markings denoted humble origins. But his territory had expanded to an impressive size.

And he was making a play for me!

I had no doubt he would be back again. Not tonight, of course. That would be too obvious. But . . . tomorrow?

When Chogyal arrived in the corridor from work a short while later, Lasya seized his hand and led him out to see where I was sitting.

"Nice to see you outside, HHC!" Scooping me up, he tickled me under the chin. "Back to normal."

I was experiencing many things at that moment. Normal, however, wasn't one of them.

The next day I could barely wait for Lasya to arrive in the afternoon. I had spent all morning grooming myself so that my thick, white pelt positively glistened. Ears thoroughly washed and whiskers shimmering, I had also performed the cello with particular vigor—much more *allegro vivo* than *adagio*, for those of you familiar with Dvořák's famous concerto.

No sooner had Lasya opened the door than I was out. I returned to the wall in a manner that tried to convey I had found myself there casually, almost accidentally. Once again, a soccer match was in full swing on the field below. From the rooms behind me there came the by-now-familiar sounds of family life. Lasya spent a few minutes sitting nearby, reading a schoolbook, before running back inside.

Out of the corner of my eye, I saw it. The shadow appeared on the 40-gallon drum. Getting up, I stretched first my front paws, then my back with luxuriant insouciance before hopping off the wall and making as if to go inside.

As I'd very much hoped, this proved too much for my admirer.

Noiselessly, he slipped from the drum and walked in such a way that our paths must cross. At the accepted distance from each other, we paused. For the first time, I looked directly into those glowing, amber eyes.

"Haven't we met somewhere before?" he asked, opening with the most clichéd pick-up line in history.

"I don't think so." I tried to inflect just the right amount of encouragement into my voice, without seeming easy.

"I'm sure I've seen you before."

I knew precisely where he'd seen me but had no intention of telling him how enthralled I'd been by the glimpse of him.

Not right now, at least.

"There are a few Himalayans about," I replied, confirming my impeccable, if undocumented, breeding. "Is this your territory?"

"All the way up to Jokhang," he said. "And down the main street to the market stalls."

The market stalls were one block short of my own preferred destination. "What about Café Franc?" I asked.

"Are you crazy? The guy there *hates* cats."

"Best cuisine in the Himalayas, according to *Hayder's Food Guide*," I responded coolly.

He blinked. *Had he never met an uptown cat before?* I wondered.

"How would you ever get near . . . ?"

"You know that saying 'It's who you know that counts'?"

He nodded.

"Not true," I smiled enigmatically. "Should be 'It's who knows *you* that counts.'"

For a while he paused, staring. I could see the curiosity in his eyes.

"Have you any advice for a tabby from the wrong side of town?" he ventured.

Oh, so sweet!

"'Then wear the gold hat, if that will move her,'" I began, quoting the epigraph from the book Tenzin believed to be America's finest novel—*The Great Gatsby*. "If you can bounce high, bounce for her, too, / Till she cry 'Lover, gold-hatted, high-bouncing lover, / I must have you!'"

He twitched his nose pensively. "Where did that come from?"

"A book I know."

He began to walk away.

"You're going?" I called, marveling again at his muscular poise.

"Off to get a hat," he replied.

There was no sign of him the following morning, but I felt sure I would see him again that afternoon. Never had I felt such romantic delirium, such a giddying, combustible mix of yearning and apprehension and inexplicable animal magnetism. I was so preoccupied that morning that I barely noticed when Chogyal arrived home at lunchtime instead of in the evening. I paid little attention when he produced the carrying cage from under his bed. It wasn't until he'd lifted me into it that I realized what was happening.

"The painters finished their work early," he explained, as though I should be delighted at what was happening. "Knowing how unhappy you were to be here, I thought you'd want to return as soon as you could."

Unceremoniously, I was carted back to Jokhang.

There was no doubt that the redecoration had been a great success. The familiar rooms now gleamed with fresh paint, the fixtures were polished to a high gloss, and everything was as it had been before, but cleaner and refurbished. The only change made had been especially for me: two rectangular cushions had been covered in taupe-colored fleece and placed on the windowsill for my comfort.

Tenzin made a great fuss over me on my return, the scent of his freshly carbolic-washed hands a pungent reminder that I was home. My favorite brand of cat food was presented for my delectation. That afternoon, as His Holiness's staff went home for the day, leaving me in peace, I should have been content that my trauma in the high-density suburb of McLeod Ganj was behind me.

Only I wasn't.

I so wanted to be back there! I ached for tiger puss! What were the chances of us meeting again if I remained in my ivory tower at Jokhang? Would he think my sudden absence meant I had no interest in him? A tabby of his leonine magnificence would have quite a following. What if he gave up on me before we even had a chance?

As I thought about my time at Chogyal's, which took on the quality of a remembered dream, I also had to admit what a fool I had been to spend three whole days under the duvet. Such a missed opportunity! What a waste! I could only imagine what might have happened if I had emerged on day one, instead of day four. What experiences I could have had, and how the relationship with the cat of my dreams might have developed. Instead, I had robbed myself of that opportunity with my ridiculous self-pity.

The Dalai Lama arrived home the next day. He only needed to step into the room, and all was well once again. Relationship angst and self-recrimination—all such trauma seemed utterly irrelevant now that His Holiness was here. Before he said so much as a word, his presence of blissful tranquility seemed to dissolve negative thoughts of all kinds, leaving only an abiding feeling of profound well-being.

Led by Tenzin and Chogyal through his redecorated chambers, the Dalai Lama beamed with delight. "Very good! Excellent!" he kept saying, as they pointed out the new brass doorknobs and improved security measures.

As soon as they had gone, he came over to stroke me. I felt a familiar glow of happiness as he looked into my eyes and whispered a few mantras.

"I know you've had a difficult time," he said after a while. "Your good friend Mrs. Trinci is coming to make lunch. I am sure she will have something delicious just for you."

Even if I had never heard of His Holiness's guest that day, I would have realized he was someone very special, for along with the delicate fragility of the small, elderly man in monk's robes, there was a remarkable power in his poise. It seemed that his travel plans had been disrupted by a trade union strike in France. As the Dalai Lama led him to a comfortable armchair, he sympathized with his visitor on the challenges of travel.

But Thich Nhat Hanh—pronounced Tick Nyut Han—Zen master, teacher, beloved guru, and author of many amazing books, shrugged off the difficulties. "Who knows what opportunities may arise as a result of the delays? I'm sure you are familiar with the Zen story of the farmer and his horse?"

His Holiness gestured for him to go on.

"The story is set in a bygone era in Japan, when a horse was not simply a horse, it was also a measure of wealth."

The Dalai Lama nodded. By now, Thich Nhat Hanh had my full attention, too.

"This farmer acquired his very first horse, and all the local villagers came around to congratulate him. 'How proud you must be to own such a magnificent horse!' they all said.

"But the farmer, understanding something about the importance of equanimity, simply smiled and said, 'We'll see.'

"Soon afterward, the horse broke out of the paddock and ran into the countryside. The villagers commiserated with the farmer. 'What a terrible tragedy! What a great loss! How is it possible to recover from such a thing?'

"Again, the farmer simply smiled and said, 'We'll see.'

"Less than a week passed, and the farmer woke to find that the horse had returned—accompanied by two wild horses. With the greatest of ease he led them into the paddock and closed the gate behind them. The villagers could hardly believe what happened. 'This is amazing good fortune! A cause for great celebration! Who could have believed such a thing was possible?'

"Of course, the farmer only smiled and said, 'We'll see.'

"His son began the work of breaking in the two wild horses. It was dangerous work, and during the course of it, he was thrown from one of the horses and broke his leg. This happened shortly before harvest, and without his son's help, the farmer faced a great challenge in collecting his crops. 'How difficult is your hardship,' the villagers told him. 'Losing your son's help at a time like this—there could be few greater misfortunes.'

"'We'll see,' is all the farmer said.

"A few days later, the Imperial Army sent troops to every village to round up fit, able-bodied young men. The Emperor had decided to go to war and was rallying the troops. But because the farmer's son had a broken leg, he was excused from service."

Thich Naht Hanh smiled. "So it goes on."

His Holiness looked at him with an appreciative smile. "A beautiful illustration."

"'Yes,'" agreed his visitor. "So much better than constantly reacting to change as if we are caught up in some kind of egocentric melodrama. Up and down like a roller coaster.'"

"Indeed," said the Dalai Lama. "We forget that it's only a matter of time before there is change—and, once again, a shift in perspective."

As much as it pains me to admit it, while listening to the conversation between these two great spiritual leaders, I found it hard to avoid reacting to the recent changes in my own circumstances. How furious I'd been with poor Chogyal when all he wanted to do was take care of me. At the time, I'd even imagined him to be like a murderous revolutionary!

Then there was my subsequent reaction—wallowing in bed for three days. How pathetic had that been? I already knew about the opportunity I had missed by burying myself under Chogyal's duvet.

Egocentric melodrama. If I were to look at myself with unflinching but compassionate honesty, would this not accurately describe the way I spent so much of my life?

"Very often," His Holiness was saying, "when I meet people—business leaders, entertainers, and others— they tell me that what seemed to be the worst thing that could ever happen to them turned out, with the benefit of hindsight, to be the very best."

"We are forced to forge a new path," said Thich Nhat Hanh. "One that may lead to greater congruence and fulfillment, if we allow it."

"Yes, yes," agreed His Holiness.

"Even when circumstances turn for the very worst," continued his visitor, "we can still find fresh opportunities."

The Dalai Lama looked pensive for a moment before he said, "The darkest moment in my life was having to leave Tibet. If China hadn't invaded our country, I would still be in Lhasa. But because of the invasion, I am here, and many other monks and nuns came, too. And in the past fifty years, the Dharma has spread throughout the world. I think it has made a useful contribution."

"I'm quite sure of it," replied Thich Nhat Hanh. "It is probably because of that event fifty years ago that we're meeting here today."

And that I am HHC, I thought.

And that you, dear reader, are holding this book.

That evening, with a belly full of Mrs. Trinci's delicious diced chicken liver, I sat on my newly cushioned sill, looking out at the green light glowing on the other side of the square. A gentle breeze carried the subtle fragrance of pine forests and lush rhododendron, along with the haunting chants of monks at prayer.

I found myself looking at the empty rock on which I'd first seen the tiger tabby. My tiger tabby. The one I very much hoped . . . *Hold on a minute*, I checked myself. Was this not a prime case of egocentric melodrama?

I was rather pleased that I had caught myself before going any further. And then I realized that being rather pleased with oneself also probably falls into the category of egocentric melodrama.

Oh, this Buddhist mind training! Can't we deceive ourselves about anything? Not even a teensy weensy bit?

I remembered Thich Nhat Hanh: his poise, his strength, his simplicity.

I stared out meditatively into the darkness, at the green light burning at the other end of the square.

We'll see.

CHAPTER EIGHT

If you are an especially astute observer of the feline condition, you may have gleaned a deeply personal insight about me. Not one I have consciously tried to convey. But like it or not, a writer betrays herself subliminally, not just in the words on the page but by leaving behind other subtle clues. A trail of psychological breadcrumbs, if you will, or perhaps, more accurately, a trail of flaked salmon. Ideally garnished with dill, or drizzled in a light but tangy dijonnaise.

Of course, you may not be reading this book in an environment that lends itself to forensic analysis. That is why I'm just going to come out with it and tell you the straightforward truth, which is—and it isn't easy to bring myself to this confession—that I am a cat who enjoys her food. And when I say enjoy, I am not, regrettably, talking about being a gourmet.

I, dear reader, am a glutton.

I know, I know—it *is* hard to believe, isn't it? You wouldn't think of it to look at me, with my chocolate-box good looks and blue-eyed sophistication. But my lustrous pelt conceals a stomach that, in the past at least, was too large to be healthy and that used me as its slave.

I am certainly not proud to have been so much in thrall to food. Is there any culture on Earth that admires the greedy guts, the sybarite, the unfettered hedonist? But before you rush to judgment, let me ask you this: Have you ever tried to imagine what it would be like to spend a day in the life of a cat?

There's no thrilling anticipation of the day's first cup of coffee, something I see written on the faces of Café Franc customers in the mornings. Nor the eye-closing delight of that first swallow of sauvignon blanc in the evening. We cats have no access to everyday mood-enhancing substances. Apart from humble cat-nip, there is no pharmaceutical refuge if we're suffering from boredom, depression, existential crisis, or even an everyday headache.

All we have is food.

The question is, at what point does enjoying one's sustenance turn from a healthy pleasure into a life-threatening obsession?

In my own case, I remember that day quite clearly.

His Holiness had been in town for more than six weeks without travel, during which his days had been filled with VIPs, some of whom were entertained at lunch. Mrs. Trinci had been a constant, operatic presence in the Jokhang kitchen, striving, with each day's performance, to reach new heights of perfection.

Through all this she never forgot the needs of The Most Beautiful Creature That Ever Lived. Not only was I treated to a constant supply of delicacies, but over time I also collected an ever-growing list of new appellations. *Dolce mio*—my sweet—she'd coo, holding me to her generous bosom and kissing my neck. *Tesorino*— little treasure—she'd croon, setting a bountiful dish of diced chicken liver before me. For Mrs. Trinci, food was a physical manifestation of love, and she was effusively generous with both.

I established something of a routine. Breakfast would be provided in our private quarters, prepared for the Dalai Lama. Then, around midmorning, I'd head down to Café Franc, where Jigme and Ngawang Dragpa were at work on the lunchtime menu. Prepared by noon, the first and finest morsels of the *menu du jour* were reserved for Rinpoche. I'd eat my meal with relish before sleeping it off for an hour or so on the top shelf. By the time I made my appearance at Jokhang between 3 and 4 P.M., Mrs. Trinci would be finishing up in the kitchen. As I hopped up on the kitchen bench, all it took was a single meow, and she'd bring me a meal, along with bountiful reassurances of my refined good looks, charm, intelligence, breeding, and any other of my numberless superior qualities that struck her at that particular moment.

All of this would have been enough—some would say more than enough—to satisfy the most discerning feline palate. But to repeat that question to which both philosophers and financial advisers devote so much of their energy: how much is enough?

This brings me to the day that I began down the slippery slope from gourmet to gourmand.

I was making my way up the hill from Café Franc, where I had indulged in a particularly generous serving of roast duck à l'orange. Almost certainly because of this, climbing the hill was more of a struggle than usual, and, for the first time, I paused on the pavement outside Cut Price Bazaar.

It so happened that Mrs. Patel, proprietor of the establishment, was sitting on a stool by the door and immediately recognized me as His Holiness's Cat. In a state of high excitement, she ordered her daughter to fetch me a saucer of milk from the back of the shop and urged me not to continue until I'd lapped up enough to gather my strength. Not wishing to cause offense, I indulged her.

As I did, Mrs. Patel sent her daughter to the grocer next door for a small tin of tuna, which she tipped onto a saucer as a further offering. I am not in the habit of accepting food from complete strangers, but I had observed Mrs. Patel many times before. A stout matriarch who spent a lot of time talking to passersby, she seemed a kind-hearted and gentle woman. As she set the saucer down, the delicious, briny tang of tuna made my nostrils flare.

Just a couple of mouthfuls, I thought, *to show I was willing.*

The following afternoon on my way up the hill, even before I'd reached Cut Price Bazaar, Mrs. Patel had milk and tuna waiting. A one-off indulgence began to take the form of a more insidious habit.

Worse was to follow.

Only days later, a benevolent Mrs. Patel intercepted me on my way down to Café Franc. Munching on a piece of naan bread stuffed with chicken, she extracted a few choice pieces for me—a midmorning snack that soon became routine.

"Cats know what's good for them" is a phrase I sometimes hear. "A cat will only eat when it's hungry" is another. Sadly, dear reader, this simply isn't true! Although I didn't realize it at the time, I had started on a perilous road to unhappiness.

Up at Jokhang, the stream of visitors seemed to be increasing. Last-minute schedule changes and long-distance telephone calls from the four corners of the world led to even more guests making the journey from Indira Gandhi Airport to McLeod Ganj. As always, Mrs. Trinci was diligent in matching cuisine to clients. Whether it was *krasnye blini* for the Russian guests or *dulce de leche* for the Argentineans, nothing was spared to surprise and delight His Holiness's visitors.

But who would ever forget the raspberry sorbet she planned for the extremely famous Indian medical doctor, public speaker, and writer who was visiting from California? Not any of the Dalai Lama's staff. Certainly not Mrs. Trinci herself.

The visitor was the third high-profile visitor in a week, after two kitchen experiences that had sorely tried Mrs. Trinci's limited patience. The first had involved an overnight refrigeration failure in the main kitchen—an inexplicable but disastrously timed event. Half the produce in the fridge had been ruined, demanding frantic last-minute visits to the market, grocers, and specialty shops to find replacements. To say that Mrs. Trinci was in a state of nervous decline by the end of the afternoon would not be going too far.

Two days later, no sooner had the main course gone on the gas rings than the fuel cut out. The tanks supplying the kitchen had emptied. There were no replacements. Runners were sent to the Namgyal Monastery kitchen to round up all available electric cookers, creating a hiatus that was, as far as the head chef was concerned, unforgivable.

Could it happen a third time in a row? Mrs. Trinci had done her utmost to make sure not. This time the gas was checked. The staff fridge upstairs, temporarily used while a replacement was on its way, had been thoroughly examined, its contents checked and double-checked. Every ingredient and utensil in the kitchen had been subjected to a rigor never before seen. Nothing was going to make this lunch go wrong.

And it didn't.

At least, not to begin with. Well ahead of schedule, Mrs. Trinci brought out the chocolate zucchini cake and carob nut balls that she'd prepared overnight for dessert. Anxious, drawn, and laboring under the superstition that bad things always came in threes, Mrs. Trinci arrived soon after His Holiness had gone to a midmorning appointment in the temple. She was leaving nothing to chance.

The asparagus niçoise was soon plated, the basmati safely consigned to the rice cooker and the vegetables to the grill. It was time to begin the coconut green beans.

But on opening bags of beans from the fridge upstairs, Mrs. Trinci discovered that they had spoiled. Somehow, as they were transferred from kitchen fridge to staff fridge, they hadn't been thoroughly checked. While the top layer was all right, beneath it many of the beans were limp and slimy. They simply wouldn't do.

Mrs. Trinci's features became more foreboding than the monsoon clouds that rolled across the Kangra Valley. Barking at the three hapless monks who'd been assigned to kitchen duty that day, she sent two to the market to find replacement beans, the other to Namgyal Monastery for emergency staff. Stressed, snapping, gold bracelets clashing every time she shook her arms, Mrs. Trinci took the bean oversight as a bad omen of worse to come.

Which it surely was.

The two assistants still hadn't returned from the market with replacement beans. The clock was ticking. The third assistant had failed to find any replacement helpers at Namgyal. Mrs. Trinci roared at him to ask upstairs. This is how His Holiness's executive assistant Chogyal found himself in the unlikely role of *sous chef* for as long as it took for Mrs. Trinci's full complement of staff to be restored.

His first task was to fetch the raspberries from the staff fridge, to begin preparation of an Ayurvedic raspberry sorbet.

"There are no raspberries," he reported, when he returned to the kitchen after a few minutes.

"Not possible. I checked last night. The red bag in the freezer." Mrs. Trinci jangled percussively as she gestured for him to return upstairs. "The red bag. *SACCHETTO ROSSO!*"

But it was no good.

"They're definitely not there," he confirmed on his return a short while later. "No red bag."

"Merda!" Mrs. Trinci slammed a drawer she had open back into its cabinet, unleashing a jangle of cutlery before storming upstairs. "Watch the vegetables under the grill!"

No one in the kitchen could avoid the heavy footfall on the staircase, or the staccato of her heels as she strode across the staff kitchen, or her howl of exasperation as she confirmed the terrible truth for herself.

"What's happened?" she demanded on her return. Face flushed to puce and eyes blazing, she poured the collective frustrations of the past week into this particular moment, a sabotage so shocking that she was still reeling from disbelief.

"They were there last night. I made sure. Now, *nulla, niente*—nothing! Where are they?"

"I'm sorry." Chogyal shook his head. "I have no idea."

His relaxed shrug did nothing to placate her.

"You work up there. You *must* know."

"The staff kitchen—"

"I had strict instructions: they mustn't be touched. They can't be replaced. I ordered them especially from Delhi. Not like that, *stupido!*" Mrs. Trinci pushed Chogyal away from the grill, where he was turning the zucchini too slowly for her liking and grabbed the tongs from his hand. "I don't have all day!"

She seized each vegetable, flipping it over and slapping it on the grill. "What must I do? Send out the monks of Namgyal to look for raspberries?"

Chogyal wisely decided to keep quiet.

"Phone every restaurant in town?" she continued, fury building. "Ask our VIP guest to buy some on his way through Delhi?"

Finished at the grill, Mrs. Trinci turned. "I am asking"—she brandished the tongs threateningly in Chogyal's face—"what am I to do?"

Chogyal knew that whatever he said would be wrong. Cornered and compliant, he opted for the obvious: "Not worry about the raspberry sorbet."

"Not worry?!" It was as though he had thrown high-octane fuel on a barely contained fire. "*Incredibile!* Whenever I try to do something really special, something above the mediocre, you people sabotage it."

Her back to the door, Mrs. Trinci couldn't see what caused Chogyal sudden concern. Far greater concern than the missing raspberries. "Mrs. Trinci—" he tried to interject.

But she was in full, Wagnerian flow. "First, it's the unreliable facilities—the fridge. Then it's the gas supply. How am I supposed to cook without a stove? Now, *porca miseria*—damn it—I have people stealing my ingredients!"

"Mrs. Trinci, please!" Chogyal pleaded, a half smile accompanied by an anxious frown. "Harsh speech!"

"Don't you 'harsh speech' me!" The ride of the Valkyries was nothing compared to Mrs. Trinci in full flight. "What kind of idiot would use the only bag of raspberries in the whole of Jokhang the day before a VIP lunch?" White flecks appeared at the sides of her mouth. "What selfish fool, what *imbecile,* would do such a thing?!"

Venting her fury on the unfortunate Chogyal, she didn't expect an answer. But through the maelstrom, a reply came nevertheless.

"It was me," a voice said softly behind her.

Mrs. Trinci wheeled around to find the Dalai Lama looking at her with immense compassion.

"I am sorry. I didn't know they were not to be used," he apologized. "We will have to do without them. Come and see me after lunch."

In the middle of the kitchen, the deep, red color in Mrs. Trinci's face rapidly drained away. She gaped like a fish, her mouth moving but no sound coming out.

Bringing his palms together at his heart, His Holiness bowed briefly. As Mrs. Trinci convulsed in the kitchen, he turned to Tenzin, who was accompanying him.

"This . . . sorbet, what is it exactly?" he asked, after they'd left the kitchen.

"A dessert, usually," said Tenzin.

"Made from raspberries?"

"You can make it in a variety of flavors," Tenzin explained. After they had walked a little farther, he added, "Actually, I think Mrs. Trinci was planning to offer it as a palate cleanser, between courses."

"A palate cleanser." Was that a glint of amusement in the Dalai Lama's eyes as he mulled over the concept? "The mind of anger is a strange thing, is it not, Tenzin?"

Later that afternoon Mrs. Trinci presented herself in His Holiness's room. From the cushioned comfort of my sill, I watched as she arrived, distraught and apologetic, awash in tears within moments of arrival.

His Holiness began by reassuring her that the guest had been highly complimentary about the lunch, especially the carob nut balls, which had reminded him of a family recipe.

But Mrs. Trinci knew that the Dalai Lama hadn't asked her up there to talk about carob nut balls. Tears pouring from her amber eyes and mascara running, she confessed to having a bad temper, saying unforgivable things, lashing out at Chogyal and anyone else who was there at the time. As she stood there sobbing, His Holiness held her hand for a long while before saying, "You know, my dear, crying isn't necessary."

Lifting a perfumed handkerchief to her face, Mrs. Trinci was startled by this notion.

"It is good, very good, to acknowledge a problem with anger," he continued.

"I've been high strung my whole life," she said.

"Sometimes we know we need to change our behavior. But it requires some sort of shock for us to *realize* we must change. Starting now."

"*Sì*." Mrs. Trinci gulped down another wave of tears. "But how?"

"Begin by considering the advantages of practicing patience and the disadvantages of not practicing it," the Dalai Lama told her. "When one is angry, the first person to suffer is oneself. No one who is angry has a happy, peaceful mind."

Mrs. Trinci looked at him intently with red-rimmed eyes.

"We also need to think about the impact on others. When we say hurtful things we don't really mean, we can create deep wounds that can't be healed. Think of all the rifts between friends and within families, divisions that have led to a complete breakdown in the relationship, all because of a single angry outburst."

"I know!" Mrs. Trinci wailed.

"Next, we ask ourselves, where is this anger coming from? If the true cause of anger is the fridge or the gas or the lack of raspberries, then why isn't everyone else angry at these things? You see, the anger isn't coming from out there. It's coming from our mind. And that is a good thing, because we can't control everything around us in the world, but we can learn to control our own mind."

"But I've always been an angry person," confessed Mrs. Trinci.

"Are you angry right now?" asked His Holiness.

"No."

"What does that tell you about the nature of an angry mind?"

For a long while Mrs. Trinci looked out the window at the temple rooftop, where the late afternoon sun had set the dharma chakra wheel and deer statue ablaze in gold. "I suppose that it comes and goes."

"Exactly. It is not permanent. It is not part of you. You cannot say, 'I've always been an angry person.' Your anger arises, abides, and passes, just like anyone else's. You may experience it more than others. And each time you give in to it, you feed the habit and make it more likely you will feel it again. Wouldn't it be better, instead, to decrease its power?"

"Of course. But I can't stop myself. I don't set out to get angry. It just happens."

"Tell me, are there some places, some situations, in which you are more likely to get angry than others?"

Mrs. Trinci's reply was instant: "The kitchen." She pointed downstairs.

"Very good," the Dalai Lama said, clapping his hands together with a smile. "From now on, Jokhang kitchen is no longer an ordinary place for you. It is, instead, a Treasure House.

"Think of it," His Holiness continued, "as a place where you will find many precious opportunities that are not available to you anywhere else."

Mrs. Trinci was shaking her head. *"Non capisco.* I don't understand."

"You agree that the anger you experience is at least partly coming from within, yes?"

"Sì."

"And that it will be very beneficial to you—and everyone else—if you can gradually get rid of it?"

"Sì."

"For this to happen, you need opportunities to practice the opposing force, which is patience. Such opportunities will not often be provided by your friends. But you will find many of them here at Jokhang."

"Sì, sì!" She smiled ruefully.

"This is why you can call it a Treasure House. It offers *many* opportunities to cultivate patience and conquer anger. There is a word for this way of thinking." His Holiness's brow furrowed in concentration. *"Reframing,* we call it. Yes. Like that."

"But what if I . . . fail?" Her voice was shaky.

"You keep trying. There are no instant results for a long-standing habit. But step by step you will definitely progress if you see the advantage."

He looked at her anxious expression for a while before saying, "It helps if you have a calm mind. For that, meditation is most useful."

"But I'm not a Buddhist."

The Dalai Lama chuckled. "Meditation does not belong to Buddhists. People from every tradition meditate, and those who have no tradition benefit from it, too. You are a Catholic, and the Benedictine order has some most useful teachings on meditation. Perhaps you can try?"

As Mrs. Trinci's audience came to an end, they stood.

"One day"—His Holiness took her hand and looked deep into her eyes—"perhaps you will see today as a turning point."

Not trusting herself to speak, Mrs. Trinci only nodded as she dabbed her eyes with a handkerchief.

"When our understanding of something deepens to the point that it changes our behavior, in the Dharma we call this a *realization*. Perhaps today you have made a realization?"

"*Sì, sì,* Your Holiness." Emotion tugged at her lips. "I certainly have."

"Remember the words of the Buddha: 'Though one man may conquer a thousand men a thousand times in battle, he who conquers himself is the greatest warrior.'"

My own realization occurred only a few weeks later.

I should have heeded the first warning—a remark I overheard Tenzin make to Chogyal when I strolled into our office one day.

"HHC is filling out," he said. It was typical Tenzin, an observation so oblique that I had only the vaguest idea what it actually meant, so I couldn't possibly take offense.

No diplomatic training was needed when I returned to Jokhang kitchen the following week for dinner courtesy of Mrs. Trinci.

An unfamiliar air of serenity had pervaded the kitchen on every one of Mrs. Trinci's visits since the Raspberry Sorbet Crisis. Not only did calm prevail that afternoon but Mrs. Trinci had even brought in a CD player from which the heavenly Sanctus chorus of Fauré's *Requiem* floated through the afternoon.

Walking into the kitchen, I greeted her with a friendly meow. I didn't jump onto the counter for the simple reason that I knew I wouldn't make it. So I looked at it instead.

Attentive as ever, Mrs. Trinci picked me up.

"Oh, poor little *dolce mio*, you can't jump up any more!" she exclaimed, smooching me demonstratively. "It's because you've put on so much weight."

I've *what*?

"You're overeating."

She can't be serious! Was this any way to talk to The Most Beautiful Creature That Ever Lived? To Tesorino? To Cara Mia?

"You've become a real piggly-wiggly."

I could hardly believe what I was hearing. The very idea was preposterous.

Piggly-wiggly? *Me?!*

I would have bitten deep into that tender spot between her thumb and index finger if it weren't for the succulent wonder of the lamb shanks in rich gravy that she placed in front of me. Lapping up the piquant sauce, I was instantly engrossed in the savory stickiness of it. Mrs. Trinci's bizarre and cruel remarks went completely out of my head.

An even greater humiliation was needed for me to face up to my expanding problem. Returning from a morning visit to the temple with His Holiness, I started up the stairs to our private quarters. Because my hind legs are so wobbly, I need to make this ascent at some speed. But in recent weeks, achieving the required velocity had become more and more of a challenge.

That morning, as it happened, it was a challenge too big.

As I leaped up the first few steps, I could sense that my usual energy was failing me. I made it to steps two and three, but instead of accelerating, something seemed to be holding me back. The usual buildup of momentum just wasn't happening.

At the critical moment, when I was about to reach the midpoint of the flight, instead of sprawling on the landing in a safe, if undignified heap, I found myself in midair, paws flailing desperately for contact. In surreal slow motion, I was tumbling backward and onto my side. I landed heavily, half on one step, half on the step below. Then, lurching lopsided and backward down the staircase, I made a terrifying and ignominious descent, only coming to a halt at His Holiness's feet.

Within moments the Dalai Lama was carrying me to our room. The vet was summoned. A towel was draped over His Holiness's desk, and I was subjected to a full examination. Dr. Guy Wilkinson didn't take long to conclude that while I was physically unharmed by the fall, and in every other respect the very model of good health, there was one particular area in which my health was seriously off kilter: I was carrying far too much weight.

How much was I being fed every day? he wanted to know.

That was a question none of His Holiness's staff could fully answer and not one I cared to respond to directly. Humiliated enough by the tumble, I had no wish to embarrass myself further by revealing the full extent of my uncurbed appetite.

But the truth came out.

Tenzin made a few well-directed phone calls, and by the end of the day, he reported to the Dalai Lama that in addition to the two meals a day I was supplied at Jokhang, I was eating three elsewhere.

A new regime was soon agreed on. Henceforth, Mrs. Trinci and Café Franc were directed to feed me half portions. I was to receive no food at all from Mrs. Patel. In the course of a few hours, my daily regime had been subjected to drastic and permanent change.

How did I feel about all of this? Had I been asked about my eating habits, I would have admitted that they should be improved. I would have readily conceded that yes, five meals a day was an excessive amount for one small—but not small enough—cat. I had known all along that I should cut down. But my knowledge had been intellectual until my humiliating tumble. Only then did that understanding become a *realization* that would change my behavior.

Life, post-tumble, would never be the same again.

That night, in the cozy darkness of bed, I felt His Holiness's hand reach out. All it took was his touch, and I'd purr with contentment.

"It's been a hard day, little Snow Lion," he whispered. "But things will get better from here. When we see for ourselves there is a problem, change becomes much easier."

And indeed it did. After the initial shock of smaller meal portions and the absence of any food at all outside Cut Price Bazaar, it was only a matter of days before I began to feel less lethargic. Within weeks, there was a new spring to my wobbly step.

Soon, I was again able to hop up on the kitchen bench. And never again did I tumble down the stairs to our quarters at Jokhang.

One Friday morning, a rectangular polystyrene box addressed to Mrs. Trinci arrived at Jokhang by courier. It was taken directly to the kitchen, where she was preparing a meal for the prime minister of India to the accompaniment of Andrea Bocelli. Surprised by the unexpected delivery, she called out to that day's *sous chef*, "Bring me a knife to open this, will you, Treasure?"

It was the term she now typically used—only sometimes through gritted teeth. While her effusive manner was much the same as it always had been, her anger arose more in the form of lightning flashes of irritation than in volcanic eruptions.

And in a curious way, it seemed that she was already being rewarded for her self-restraint. Just recently she'd heard from her daughter, Serena, who had trained as a chef in Italy before spending several years working at a variety of Michelin-starred restaurants in Europe. Mrs. Trinci was beyond pleased to learn that Serena had decided she'd had enough of Europe for a while. In just a few weeks she would be back home in McLeod Ganj.

Knife in hand, Mrs. Trinci sliced the wrapping tape and protective covering of the mysterious delivery, opening the package to reveal a frosted plastic container of bright red liquid—and an envelope with her name on it.

"Dear Mrs. Trinci," read the short note. "My grateful thanks for the wonderful Ayurvedic meal I enjoyed recently with His Holiness. I was sorry to hear that you were unable to prepare the raspberry sorbet you had planned. So I hope you enjoy the enclosed, made according to a favorite Ayurvedic recipe. May it bring you and your guests good health and much happiness."

"*Mamma mia!*" Mrs. Trinci stared at the letter. "How amazing! What generosity!"

Moments later she was opening the lid and sampling the contents.

"Exquisite!" she pronounced, eyes closed as she ran the mixture ruminatively around her mouth. "So much better than I could have made."

She picked up the container to see how much there was. "And it will do perfectly as a palate-cleanser today."

Later, I heard Tenzin and Chogyal discussing that day's lunch. The great political accord of the occasion had been assisted, in no small measure, by the wonderful food. The prime minister, unable to believe that His Holiness's cook was not Indian, had called her upstairs to offer his congratulations. Apparently, he had gone into raptures over the raspberry sorbet.

"Isn't it interesting the way these things work out?" Tenzin remarked to Chogyal. "Mrs. Trinci is so much calmer and more contented these days."

"That's for sure!" Chogyal's agreement was heartfelt.

"And of all the days she could have offered it, serving raspberry sorbet today was a masterstroke."

"Indeed it was."

CHAPTER NINE

"She's doing *what?*" Tenzin's voice sounded tense as he spoke on the phone. I raised my head from where I was dozing on the filing cabinet behind him. It was unlike Tenzin, the consummate diplomat, to react to anything with such strength.

Across the desk, I saw surprise flicker across Chogyal's face.

"Yes, of course." Tenzin reached out to the silver-framed photograph on his desk. It showed a young woman in a black dress playing the violin with a full orchestra behind her. His wife, Susan, had been a highly accomplished musician when they'd met years ago at Oxford University. That was before Tenzin accepted the job of a lifetime as His Holiness's adviser on diplomatic matters. And well before the arrival of their son, Peter, and daughter, Lauren. Lauren was 14 years old—an age, Tenzin had once confided to Chogyal, designed to try the patience of parents. I guessed that the telephone call must be about her.

"We'll discuss it later." Tenzin hung up.

As is so often the way, Tenzin was having a tough time all around. On top of all his usual pressing responsibilities, he was also planning the relocation of His Holiness's archives, to be carried out the following week.

More than 60 years of important documentation had built up in the adjacent room, and while a lot of material had been scanned and backed up electronically, there were still many important diplomatic agreements, financial records, licenses, and other documents that needed to be retained. Tenzin had arranged for a secure room in Namgyal Monastery to be the future repository for most of these and had meticulously planned for the archives to be transferred over three consecutive days— days during which His Holiness was, unusually, receiving no visitors. That way, the disruption would be kept to a minimum.

In most organizations, tasks of this kind fall into the category of "administrative tedium." But at Jokhang, there is often an unexpected quality to the way in which even the most routine chore is undertaken, as though there is a lot more to the most pedestrian activity than meets the eye.

Relocating His Holiness's archives was just such a case in point. Tenzin had outlined his plan over a cup of tea during one of his afternoon meetings with the Dalai Lama. His Holiness had agreed and, to Tenzin's surprise, had said he would personally select the monks who were to assist with the transfer.

The following morning His Holiness returned from the day's first session at the temple with two fit and healthy young monks who were to receive instructions from Tenzin. Also with him were two wide-eyed young brother novices, Tashi and Sashi, not even in their teens, who kept fervently prostrating every time His Holiness so much as looked in their direction.

"We have our volunteers for the relocation." The Dalai Lama gestured toward the two young men. "And also two helpers to take care of HHC."

If Tenzin was at all surprised by this consideration, he gave no sign of it. What archival relocation plan did not include feline management as an integral part of it? It was true that the traffic of files through the executive assistants' office would disrupt my usual inactivity. My viewing platform would have to be moved out of the way. This is why it was decided that for the three mornings in question, I was to be taken to the visitors' room next door. A spacious, light-filled chamber with armchairs and coffee tables, a selection of daily newspapers, and a corner desk furnished with a computer. This was where people usually waited before an audience with His Holiness.

The Dalai Lama personally explained the duties he expected Tashi and Sashi to perform. I was to be carried very gently to the visitors' room and taken to a corner windowsill on which a fleece blanket had been folded and placed for my use. Two bowls containing water and biscuits respectively were to be kept clean and filled. If I wanted to go downstairs, I was to be accompanied to make sure I didn't get caught underfoot. While I was sleeping, the novices were to meditate near me, reciting the mantra "Om Mani Padme Hum."

"Above all"—His Holiness's expression was firm—"you must treat her as you would your favorite lama."

"But *you* are our favorite lama!" Sashi, the younger of the novices, burst out impetuously, bringing his palms to his heart.

"In that case"—His Holiness smiled—"treat her as if she were the Dalai Lama."

This is just what they did, with the kind of earnest reverence I usually received only at Café Franc. At the end of that first morning, returning to the executive assistant's office, I found my filing cabinet shifted to the side of the room. Like most cats, I love nothing better than a familiar scene with a slight change in orientation, so I immediately hopped up on the cabinet to look down at the room from a novel perspective.

By then I had forgotten Tenzin's raised voice on the phone from the week before, but that afternoon, as he ended a conversation with his wife, it was clear that something was troubling him.

Chogyal looked up in sympathetic inquiry.

"It's Lauren," he confirmed. "Last week, Susan walked into her room and found her sitting on her bed, looking furtive and hiding something behind her back. She pretended everything was all right. But Susan knew it wasn't.

"Lauren has been a bit strange lately. She's been tiring easily and feeling faint. She just hasn't been herself. One morning, Susan was vacuuming Lauren's room and found some rocks under her bed.

Different sizes. Susan couldn't work it out. She wondered if that was what Lauren had been hiding. But why hide rocks?

"When Susan asked her about the rocks, Lauren burst into tears. It took her a while to confess because she was embarrassed. She'd been eating rocks."

Chogyal looked astonished.

"Rocks from . . . ?"

"She felt this strange, inexplicable compulsion to go into the garden and find a stone and start chewing on it."

"Poor girl!"

"Susan took her to see the doctor. Apparently, what she has is unusual but by no means unheard of. Teenage girls sometimes crave chalk, soap, and other things because of nutritional deficiencies. In her case, a lack of iron."

"Ah!" Chogyal hardly missed a beat. "She's vegetarian?"

Tenzin nodded. "Like her mother."

"Can they give her iron supplements?"

"As a short-term measure. But on an ongoing basis the doctor says iron should come from her regular diet. He suggests lean meat, ideally beef. But she won't accept it."

"On principle?"

"She said, 'I don't want to be responsible for animals being killed! Why can't I just take an iron supplement?' Susan and I are very concerned."

"Difficult to persuade a teenager."

"Children of that age don't listen to their parents." Tenzin was shaking his head. "I am wondering about a different solution."

I discovered what that solution was two days later. It was the third and final day of the archive move. I was dozing in the visitors' room, the two novice monks chanting mantras softly beside me, when Tenzin arrived with Lauren in tow, carrying her school bag. She had finished her classes for the day, and because her mother had to go out, she had come to Jokhang to do her homework. This arrangement happened a handful of times each year. Usually, she'd sit in the office with Tenzin and Chogyal, but because of the general upheaval, Tenzin put her at the desk in the corner of the visitors' lounge.

That, at least, was the cover story.

Pulling out her books, Lauren started working on an English assignment. She was engrossed in the comprehension exercise, her face filled with delight, when half an hour later, the door to His Holiness's suite opened, and he stepped outside.

"Lauren! Good to see you!" He brought his palms to his heart and bowed to her.

She had already risen from her chair and was also bowing, before giving him a self-conscious hug. His Holiness had known her since she was born, and there was genuine warmth between them.

"How are you, my dear?"

Most of us give a polite, pro forma answer to that question. But perhaps because the Dalai Lama was asking it, or perhaps because of the way he made her feel at that particular moment, instead of the routine response she said, "I have an iron deficiency, Your Holiness."

"Oh! I am very sorry." Taking her hand, he sat on one of the sofas and gestured for her to sit beside him. "A doctor says this?"

She nodded.

"It can be treated?"

"That's what's the matter." Her eyes filled with tears. "He says I must eat meat."

"Ah, yes. You are vegetarian." He stroked her hand comfortingly. "Being vegetarian all the time is the ideal."

"I know," she agreed, unhappily.

"If, through compassion, one can abstain completely from eating the flesh of living beings, this is best. Therefore, everyone who can do this should consider it. But if, for medical reasons, you can only be vegetarian *most* of the time, then maybe you have to do this."

"Most of the time?"

He nodded. "Doctors also said I have to eat meat sometimes, for nutritional reasons."

"I didn't know that." She studied him very closely.

"Yes. I decided, even if I can't be vegetarian all the time, I will follow a vegetarian diet as much as possible but be moderate about it. Being vegetarian or non-vegetarian need not be black or white. We can find a middle ground. Sometimes eating meat for nutritional purposes, but all the time not necessary. My heartfelt wish is that everyone would consider doing the same thing."

It seemed that Lauren hadn't even considered this possibility.

"But what happens if you don't want *any* animals to be killed just so you can eat?" she asked.

"Lauren, you have a good heart! But such a thing is not possible."

"It's possible for vegetarians."

"No." His Holiness shook his head. "Not even for them."

Her brow furrowed.

"Sentient beings are killed even for a vegetarian diet. When land is cleared to make space for crops, the natural habitat is destroyed, and many smaller beings are killed. Then crops are planted, and pesticides are sprayed, killing many thousands of insects. You see, it is very difficult to avoid harming other beings, especially in relation to food."

For Lauren, who had thought that being vegetarian meant that no living beings would be harmed, this was a difficult discovery. Her certainty was being shaken.

"The doctor says I should eat lean meat, like beef. But from a compassionate point of view, if you have to eat the flesh of an animal, wouldn't it be better to eat a being like a fish?"

His Holiness nodded. "I understand what you're saying, but there are some who would say that eating a cow is better, because a single cow can provide more than one thousand meals. A fish, only one meal. Sometimes it takes many prawns, many sentient beings, for only one meal."

Lauren looked at the Dalai Lama for a long time. Eventually she said, "I didn't realize it was so complicated."

"It is a very big subject," he agreed. "You will find that some people tell you there is only one way, *this* way, which happens to be the way that they think, and that everyone else should change their views to be like them. But it is really a matter of personal choice. The important thing is to make sure our decisions are guided with compassion *and* wisdom."

She nodded earnestly.

"Before we eat any meal, vegetarian or meat, we should always remember the beings that have died so that we can eat. Their lives were just as important to them as your life is to you. Think of them with gratitude and pray that their sacrifice will be a cause for them to be reborn in a higher realm—and for you to be healthy, so that you can quickly, quickly reach full enlightenment in order to lead them to that same state."

"Yes, Your Holiness," said Lauren, leaning against him.

For a moment, the whole room was flooded with a warm glow. In the corner, near where I was dozing, the two novice monks, who had been listening to the conversation, continued to whisper their mantras.

His Holiness got up from the sofa, and as he was making his way across the visitors' room, he said, "As much as possible, it is useful to think of all other beings as being just like me. Every living being strives for happiness. Every being wants to avoid all forms of suffering. They are not just objects or things to be used for our benefit. You know, Mahatma Gandhi once said: 'The greatness of a nation and its moral progress can be judged by the way its animals are treated.' Interesting, isn't it?"

Later that afternoon I was with the Dalai Lama, occupying my usual spot on the windowsill. There was a tentative knock on the door, then the two novices made their appearance.

"You wanted to see us, Your Holiness?" Tashi, the older one asked, somewhat nervously.

"Yes, yes." The Dalai Lama opened one of the drawers of his desk and took out two sandalwood *malas*, or strings of prayer beads. "This is a small gift to thank you for looking after HHC," he said.

Each boy accepted a mala, bowing in solemn thanks.

His Holiness said a few words about the importance of mindfulness when practicing meditation, then gave them a benevolent smile.

The short audience had come to an end, but the two novices stood where they were, exchanging nervous glances.

It was only when the Dalai Lama said, "You may go," that Tashi asked in a piping voice, "Can I ask you a question, please, Your Holiness?"

"Of course," he responded, a glint in his eye.

"We heard what you said earlier today about living beings. How they are not just objects to be used."

"Yes, yes."

"We have a confession to make. A terrible thing we did."

"Yes, Your Holiness," interjected Sashi, "but it was before we became novices."

"Our family in Delhi was very poor," Tashi started to explain. "Once, we found four kittens in a back alley and sold them for sixty rupees—"

"—and two U.S. dollars," Sashi added.

"No questions asked," Tashi said.

"Perhaps they were only bought for their fur coats," Sashi ventured.

On the sill I looked up suddenly. Was I to believe what I was hearing? Were these two novices really the same unscrupulous little demons who had cruelly stolen me from the warm safety of my family home? Who had brutally wrenched my siblings and me from our mother before we were even properly weaned? Who had treated us like nothing more than merchandise? How could I forget the way they'd humiliated me, shoving me into a mud puddle, or how, when I went unsold, they'd so casually planned to destroy me?

Along with the shock, resentment welled up inside me.

But then it came to me: had it not been for them selling me, I would probably have died or been condemned to a harsh life in a Delhi slum. Instead, here I was, the Snow Lion of Jokhang.

"Yes," continued Tashi. "That last kitten was small and dirty and could hardly walk."

"We were going to throw it out," Sashi added.

"I was already wrapping it in newspaper," Tashi said. "It looked like it was almost dead."

"Then," said Sashi, "this rich official comes and gives us $2. Just like that." The thrill of the moment was still etched vividly in his mind.

Mine, too.

But their feelings about the event had undergone a metamorphosis.

"We realize what a bad thing we did." They both looked remorseful. "Just using small kittens for our own benefit."

"I see," nodded His Holiness.

"The youngest kitten especially," said Tashi. "It was very weak—"

Sashi shook his head. "We were paid all that money, but the kitten probably died."

The brothers looked at His Holiness nervously, bracing for a wrathful condemnation of their selfishness.

Only, the condemnation didn't come.

Instead, the Dalai Lama told them seriously, "In the Dharma, there is no place for guilt. Guilt is useless. It is pointless to feel bad about something in the past that we can't change. But regret? Yes. This is more useful. Do you both feel sincere regret for what you did?"

"Yes, Your Holiness," they chorused.

"You are committed to never harming a living being again in that way?"

"Yes, Your Holiness!"

"When you practice compassion in meditation, think about those small kittens and the countless other weak and vulnerable beings who need your protection and love."

His Holiness's features lightened. "As for that very weak kitten you thought might have died, I believe you will discover that she grew into a beautiful being." He gestured toward where I was sitting on the sill.

As they turned to look at me, Tashi exclaimed, "His Holiness's Cat?"

"It was one of my staff who paid you the $2. We had just returned from America, and he didn't have any rupees."

Approaching me, they stroked the back of my head and my back.

"It is very fortunate that we all now enjoy such a good home here at Namgyal Monastery," said His Holiness.

"Yes," agreed Sashi. "But it is very strange karma how we have spent the past three days looking after the same cat we once sold."

Perhaps that part wasn't so strange. The Dalai Lama is believed to be clairvoyant. I guessed that the reason he had chosen the two novices to perform their particular task had been precisely because of their past actions. He was giving them an opportunity to make amends.

"Yes, karma propels us into all kinds of unexpected situations," His Holiness said. "This is another reason we should behave with love and compassion toward all living beings. We never know in what circumstances we will meet up with them again. Sometimes even in this same lifetime."

CHAPTER TEN

Have you ever been paralyzed by indecision, dear reader? Found yourself in a situation where if, on the one hand, you do this, that, or the next, a certain result may occur, but if, on the other hand, you do something different, another better result may occur—only the chances of it happening are less likely, so perhaps you'd be better off sticking with the first course of action?

You may have imagined that we cats never get caught up in such cognitive complexity. Maybe you believed that existential overload is the unique preserve of Homo sapiens.

As it happens, nothing could be further from the truth. *Felis catus*—the domestic cat—may not have a career to build, a commercial endeavor to attend to, or any of the whirling carousel of activities that make humans such relentlessly busy beings. But there is one area in which we are startlingly similar.

I am talking, of course, about matters of the heart.

Humans may wait in desperation for a particular text message, e-mail, or phone call. We cats have different ways of communicating. The form is unimportant. All that matters is the confirmation we so desperately seek.

I was in just such a position when it came to my tabby friend. My attraction was instant, from the first moment I saw him under the green light. When we actually met, during my stay at Chogyal's, there had been an unmistakable and, I thought, mutual *frisson*. But now that I was no longer staying with Chogyal, did he know where I lived? Should I make more of an effort—say, by crossing the temple courtyard one night and exploring the shadowy netherworld beyond? Or should I remain coolly enigmatic, a feline of great mystery, and rely on him to come looking?

It was Lobsang, His Holiness's translator, who brought much-needed clarity to my situation. And, as is so often the case with these things, in the least expected way. A tall, slim Tibetan Buddhist monk in his mid-30s, Lobsang was originally from Bhutan, where he was a distant relative of the royal family. He had received a thoroughly Western education in America, graduating from Yale with a degree in Philosophy of Language and Semiotics. As well as his height and a radiant intelligence, there was something else you became aware of the moment that Lobsang stepped into a room. It was an aura of calm. He was suffused with serenity. A deep, abiding tranquility seemed to emanate from every cell of his body, affecting everyone around him.

In addition to his responsibilities as translator, Lobsang was also the unofficial head of information technology at Jokhang. Whenever computers were uncooperative, printers turned surly, or satellite receiver boxes switched to passive-aggressive mode, it was Lobsang who was called upon to apply his calm, incisive logic to the problem.

So when the main modem at Jokhang went on the blink one afternoon, it didn't take five minutes for Tenzin to summon Lobsang from his office down the corridor. After a few simple checks, Lobsang concluded that a fault in the line was the problem. Help from the phone company was summoned forthwith.

Which is how Raj Goel, technical support services representative of Dharamsala Telecom, came to be at Jokhang late that afternoon. A slight man in his mid-20s with a wiry frame and thick mop of hair, he seemed extremely disgruntled at having to provide technical support services to a customer. The cheek of it! The nerve!

Face set to a scowl, his manner brusque, he demanded to be shown the modem and the telephone lines coming into Jokhang. These were located in a small room down the corridor. Slamming his metal briefcase on a shelving unit with an angry crash, he flicked open the clasps, extracted a flashlight and a screwdriver, and was soon poking and prodding a tangle of cables, while Lobsang stood a few feet away, calmly attentive.

"Mess, this place," Raj Goel growled under his breath.

Lobsang gave the impression of not having heard the remark.

Grunting as he got to his knees and followed a particular cable to the back of the modem, the technician muttered darkly about systems integrity, interference, and other arcane matters before seizing the modem angrily, tugging a number of cables at the back, and turning it over in his hands.

As Raj Goel was venting his spleen, Tenzin happened to walk past. He met Lobsang's eyes with an expression of dry amusement.

"I'm going to have to open this," the technician told Lobsang in an accusatory tone.

His Holiness's translator nodded. "Okay."

Rummaging in his briefcase for a smaller screwdriver, Raj Goel began working on the case of the offending modem.

"No time for religion."

Was he speaking to himself? His voice seemed too bold for that.

"Superstitious nonsense," he complained a few moments later, even louder.

Lobsang was untroubled by the remarks. If anything, a smile seemed to have appeared on his lips.

But Raj Goel was spoiling for a fight. Battling with an unyielding screw as he leaned over the modem, this time he spoke in a tone that demanded a response. "What's the point of filling people's heads with silly beliefs?"

"I agree," Lobsang replied. "No point at all."

"Huh!" the other exclaimed some time later, triumphing over the obdurate screw. "But you're religious." This time he shot Lobsang a hard-eyed glance. "You're a Believer."

"I don't think of it that way at all." Lobsang emanated profound calm. After a pause, he continued. "One of the last things Buddha said to his followers was that anyone who believed a word he had taught them was a fool—unless they had tested it against their own experience."

Patches of sweat began appearing on the technician's polyester shirt. Lobsang's reaction was not the one he was after. "Sneaky words," he groused. "I see people bowing down to Buddhas in temples. Chanting prayers. What's that if it isn't blind faith?"

"Before I answer that, let *me* ask *you* something." Lobsang leaned against the door frame. "You're at Dharamsala Telecom. Two calls come in during the morning: one from a customer who accidently overturned a filing cabinet onto his modem, the other from a customer who got so angry with his wife for shopping online that he smashed their modem with a hammer. In both cases, the modems are broken and need to be repaired or replaced. Do you treat both customers the same?"

"Of course not!" scowled Raj Goel. "What has that got to do with bowing and scraping to Buddhas?"

"Quite a lot." Lobsang's easy poise couldn't have contrasted more starkly with Raj Goel's prickliness. "I'll explain why. But those two customers—"

"The one was an accident," the technician interjected, his voice rising. "The other was a deliberate act of vandalism."

"What you're saying is that intention is more important that an action itself?"

"Of course."

"So when a person bows down to a Buddha, what really matters is the intention, not the bowing?"

It was at this point that the technical support services representative began to realize he had blustered his way into a corner. Not that he was about to back out. "The intention is obvious," he argued.

Lobsang shrugged. "You tell me."

"The intention is that you are begging Buddha for forgiveness. You are hoping for salvation."

Lobsang burst out laughing. His manner was so gentle, however, that for the first time Raj Goel's indignation seemed to wane.

"I think, perhaps, you are thinking of something else," Lobsang said after a while. "Enlightened beings cannot take away your suffering or give you happiness. If they could do this, wouldn't they have done so already?"

"Then why do you bother?" The technician was shaking his head as he fiddled with the modem.

"As you have already said, the intention is important. The statue of Buddha represents a state of enlightenment. Buddhas don't need people to bow down to them. Why should they care? When we bow, we are reminding ourselves that our own natural potential is one of enlightenment."

By now, Raj Goel had the modem cover off, and he was fiddling with connections to the circuitry inside. "If you don't worship Buddha"—he tried to retain the edge to his voice, though it seemed to be becoming an effort—"what is Buddhism about?"

By now Lobsang had sufficient measure of his visitor to provide an answer to which he could relate. "The science of the mind," he said.

"Science?"

"What if someone conducted tens of thousands of hours of rigorous investigation to discover truths about the nature of consciousness? Suppose other people replicated the research over hundreds of years. How amazing would it be not just to have an intellectual understanding of the mind's potential but also to establish the most rapid and direct way to realize it? That is the science of Buddhism."

Having fiddled with the innards of the modem, Raj Goel was replacing its cover. After a while he said, "I am interested in quantum science." Then, after a moment's pause, he announced, "The modem is working, but I have to reset it, to be on the safe side. The line fault has been reported. It should be up and running within twelve hours."

Perhaps Lobsang's immensely calming presence had begun to affect him. Or maybe it was the translator's explanations that had stopped him in his tracks. But there was no further grunting or moaning as the visitor completed his work and replaced his tools.

On the way back down the corridor, as they passed Lobsang's office, the translator said, "I have something here that may be of interest." He ducked inside and took a book from one of the bookshelves lining the walls.

"*The Quantum and the Lotus.*" Raj Goel read the title before flicking the book open.

"You can borrow it if you like."

There was an inscription on the title page from one of the book's authors, Matthieu Ricard.

"It's signed," noted the visitor.

"Matthieu is a friend of mine."

"He has visited Jokhang?"

"I first met him in America," said Lobsang. "I lived there for ten years."

For the first time, Raj Goel looked at Lobsang closely. That revelation was of far greater interest to him than anything else the translator had said. Realizing your natural potential. Achieving enlightenment. Yada, yada, yada. But *lived in America for ten years*?!

"Thank you," said the visitor, slipping the book into his briefcase. "I will return it."

The following Monday afternoon I heard Raj Goel's voice coming down the corridor. As extraordinarily rude visitors to Jokhang are very rare, my curiosity drew me away from my afternoon siesta to Lobsang's visitor, who was being shown to his office.

Had the technician come to pick another fight?

But the Raj Goel who had just arrived was a changed person from the snapping and snarling technical support representative of the previous week. Without all that energizing hostility, he cut a somewhat forlorn figure, with his faded shirt and battered briefcase.

"No further problems with the phone lines?" he was confirming, as I padded into Lobsang's office behind him.

"Working perfectly, thank you." Lobsang was behind his desk.

His visitor produced the borrowed book from inside his briefcase. "This has provided an interesting perspective," he said. What he meant was, "Sorry I was so obnoxious last week."

As a graduate in semiotics, Lobsang understood this. "Good," he nodded. "I hoped you would find it stimulating." By which he meant, "Apology accepted. We all have our days."

There was a pause. Having put the book on Lobsang's desk, Raj Goel took a step back. He didn't look at

Lobsang directly but glanced around the office for a few moments as though trying to find the right words.

"So . . . you lived in America?" he asked eventually.

"Yes."

"For ten years?"

"That's right."

Another long pause. Then, "What is it like?"

Lobsang pushed back from his desk and waited till his visitor finally looked him in the eye. "Why do you want to know?"

"Because I want to go live there for a while, but my family wants me to marry," Raj Goel began.

It seemed that Lobsang's question had dislodged a blockage of some kind. Once Raj Goel started, there was no stopping him. "I have friends in New York saying 'Come and stay with us,' and I am very keen to do so, because all my life I've wanted to visit the Big Apple and earn real dollars and maybe even meet a movie star. But my parents have chosen this girl, you see, and her parents also want us to marry, and they are saying, 'America will always be there.' Also, my boss is pressuring me to go into management development training, but the loan will tie me to the company for six years and I'm feeling trapped. As it is, work pressure is already overwhelming."

After this sudden outpouring, the stillness of Lobsang's office was palpable. Lobsang gestured toward a pair of chairs in the corner. "Would you like a cup of tea?"

A short while later, the two of them were sitting together. As Lobsang sipped his tea, Raj Goel spared no detail about the conflicting pressures—pressures that were, no doubt, the real source of his disagreeable behavior the week before. He told Lobsang about the agonies of following his friends on Facebook and YouTube as they traveled around America. How his parents thought that a middle-management position with Dharamsala Telecom was the most he could ever aspire to, but he had his own, more entrepreneurial ideas. How his instincts to spread his wings were in constant tension with the loyalty he felt toward his parents, who had made great sacrifices to give him a good education.

The past few weeks in particular had been a time of great anxiety and sleepless nights. He told Lobsang how he had tried to be rational, looking at the advantages and disadvantages of each course of action.

It was at this point that my casual interest in the conversation became suddenly personal. Trying to weigh one course of action against another—that sounded familiar! Raj Goel and I were the same in this respect.

Finally, the visitor confessed the real purpose of his visit that morning: "I am hoping you can give me some advice to help me reach a decision."

Making my way toward a spare armchair, I hopped up on it and fixed Lobsang with an expression of blue clarity. I was most interested in hearing what he had to say.

"I don't have any special wisdom," said Lobsang, in the way that especially wise practitioners always do. "I have no qualities or realizations. I don't know why you think I can advise."

"But you lived in America for ten years." Raj Goel was vehement. "And . . . " Lobsang waited for him to finish. "You know about things." Raj Goel lowered his gaze as though embarrassed to be admitting this, especially to a man whose mental capacity he had questioned only a week earlier.

Lobsang simply asked him, "Do you love the girl?"

Raj Goel seemed surprised by the question. He shrugged. "I have seen a photograph of her only once."

His reply remained suspended in space for a while, like a rising wisp of smoke. "I'm told she wants children, and my parents want us to have children."

"Your friends in America. How long will they be there?"

"They have two-year visas. They plan on traveling coast to coast."

"If you want to join them, you must go—?"

"Soon."

Lobsang nodded. "What is holding you back?"

"My parents," Raj Goel retorted somewhat sharply, as though Lobsang hadn't grasped any of what he'd been saying. "The arranged marriage. My boss who wants me to—"

"Yes, yes, the management training." Lobsang's tone was skeptical.

"Why do you say it like that?"

"Like what?"

"Like you don't really believe me."

"Because I don't really believe you." Lobsang's smile was so compassionate, so gentle, that it was impossible to take offense.

"I can show you the forms," his visitor told him. "They must be handed in."

"Oh, I believe all you say about the training and the parents and the marriage. I just don't believe those are the *real* reasons you feel trapped."

Deep furrows had returned to Raj Goel's forehead. But this time they were furrows of perplexity.

"I thought you would agree that these are important responsibilities."

"What—because I am a Buddhist monk?" chided Lobsang. "Because I'm a religious person who wants to uphold the status quo? Is that why you sought my advice?"

Raj Goel looked abashed.

"You are an intelligent, inquisitive young fellow, Raj. You have been presented with the opportunity of a lifetime. A chance to become a man of the world and to get to understand a lot more not only about America but also about yourself. Why would you *not* seize this opportunity?"

Lobsang posed this as a serious question, and it was some time before his visitor answered. "Because I'm scared of what may happen?"

"Fear," said Lobsang. "An instinct that prevents many people from taking actions that they know, deep down inside, would liberate them. Like a bird in a cage whose door has been opened, we are free to go out in search of fulfillment, but fear makes us look for all kinds of reasons not to."

Raj Goel stared at the floor for a while before meeting Lobsang's eyes. "You are right," he admitted.

"The Indian Buddhist guru Shantideva had some wise words on this very subject," Lobsang said. He began to quote: "'When crows encounter a dying snake, / They will act as though they were eagles. / Likewise, if my self-confidence is weak, / I shall be injured by the slightest downfall.'

"Now is not the time to be weak or to let your fears overwhelm you, Raj. You may find that if you face your fears head-on, things may not be as bad as you think. Perhaps, after your parents get used to the idea, they won't be so disappointed. The arranged marriage can wait. Or maybe in two years' time, there can be a different match. In the meantime, there are many, many things to look forward to. I am sure you will find America an amazing place."

"I know," Raj Goel said, this time with conviction. Leaning forward in the chair, he picked up his briefcase and practically jumped up with newfound purpose. "You are definitely right! Thank you very much for your advice!"

The two men shook hands warmly.

"You may even meet a movie star," suggested Lobsang.

"Which is why I must feel the fear," Raj Goel declared with fervor, "and do it anyway!"

It is interesting how, once you have decided to strike out on a new course of action, events often transpire to help you. Not always in an obvious fashion, or immediately. And sometimes in ways you would never have considered.

That night, as inspired by Lobsang's advice as Raj Goel had been, I decided to head across the temple courtyard to where the green light burned at the end of Mr. Patel's market stall. No longer would I allow silly excuses to keep me pining on the windowsill. The fear of failure or of rejection was not for me. I wasn't some silly budgerigar sitting in a cage with an open door.

The expedition was not a success. Not only did my tabby fail to materialize, but as I casually strolled through some of the lanes, I found myself getting more and more lost. It was only thanks to a Namgyal monk who recognized me as HHC and returned me to the door of my home that the evening didn't end in a complete fiasco.

But the following afternoon, after my post-lunch siesta, I was passing out of Café Franc when who should suddenly appear at my side but my mackerel-striped admirer.

"I can't believe you just did that!" he exclaimed, referring to my brazen visit to the emporium of a supposed cat-hater.

"Oh," I said with a shrug, not only thrilled that he had appeared but also that he had done so at a moment when I possessed an almost impossible savoir faire. "It's the way you do these things."

"Where are you going?" he wanted to know.

"Jokhang," I replied.

"You're a member of the household?"

"Something like that." I would reveal the truth of my lofty status in my own time. "As it happens," I told him enigmatically, "I have an important lap to sit on in twenty minutes."

"Whose lap?"

"I couldn't possibly say. When people have an audience with the Dalai Lama, it's *completely* confidential."

The tabby's eyes widened visibly. "At least give me a clue!" he pleaded.

"My professionalism forbids it," I told him. Then, after we'd walked some distance, I added, "Let me just say that she is a blonde American talk show host."

"There are so many."

"You know, the one who is always getting her audiences to get up and dance. She's a very good dancer herself."

But the tiger tabby just wasn't getting it.

"The one married to that stunningly beautiful actress who is a patron of stray cats."

"Which stunningly beautiful actress is a patron of stray cats?"

Subtlety, I was discovering, was not my admirer's middle name.

"Let's not go there," I said, refusing to abandon all my discretion. At the same time, I didn't wish to seem completely standoffish. "Tell me, what is your name?"

"Mambo," he replied. "And yours?"

"I have a lot of names," I began.

"Pedigrees usually do."

I smiled, letting the misunderstanding pass. Isn't it only because of circumstances that my impeccable family background is not formally documented?

"But you must have a usual name."

"In my case," I replied, "they're initials. HHC."

"HHC?"

"That's right." We were approaching the gates of Jokhang.

"What do they stand for?"

"That's your homework, Mambo. You're a streetwise cat." I watched his muscled chest swell with pride. "I know you'll work it out."

I turned in the direction of Jokhang.

"How can I find you?" he called out.

"Look for me when you're under the green light that burns all night."

"I know the one."

"And bring your gold hat."

He was there the next night. I was on my sill but pretended not to see him. It wouldn't do to be that easy. I wanted to test how devoted he really was.

When he meowed two nights later, I relented and went downstairs.

"I worked it out," he told me when I was still some distance away from the stone he was sitting on—the same place he'd been when I caught my first glimpse of him.

"Worked out what?"

"His Holiness's Cat. That's who you are, isn't it?"

For a moment the whole world seemed to pause, holding its breath, waiting for the great mystery of my identity to be revealed.

"Yes, Mambo," I confirmed eventually, fixing him with my big, blue eyes. "But don't make a big thing of it."

His voice sank to a whisper. "I can't believe it. Me, from the slums of Dharamsala. You with your own initials. I mean, you're practically royalty!"

"A cat might be . . . " What could I say without seeming impossibly vain? His Holiness's Bodhicatva? Café Franc's Rinpoche? Mrs. Trinci's Most Beautiful Creature That Ever Lived? Chogyal and Tenzin's Snow Lion? (Or, heaven forbid, the driver's Mousie-Tung?) "A cat might be HHC," I said finally, "but she is still . . . very much . . . a cat."

"I hear what you're saying."

I very much doubted it. I wasn't entirely sure myself what I meant. "So what did you have in mind for tonight?"

I will, dear reader, spare you the details of all that occurred on that and subsequent nights. I am not that kind of cat. This is not that kind of book. And you are most certainly not that kind of reader!

Suffice it to say that not a day passed that I didn't, with all my heart, thank Lobsang for his words of wisdom. Shantideva, too. And Dharamsala Telecom for sending their disgruntled technical support services representative to Jokhang.

About two months after Raj Goel's visits, I was in my customary spot on the filing cabinet in the executive assistants' office when Lobsang came by.

"Something for you got caught up in our post today," Tenzin told him, flicking through some envelopes on his desk before retrieving a glossy postcard of a glamorous female celebrity.

"Raj Goel?" Lobsang scanned the card and read the signature, trying to place the name. "Oh, *that* Raj!"

"Friend?" inquired Tenzin.

"Remember the fellow from Dharamsala Telecom who came to check our line fault a couple of months ago? Turns out, he now works for one of the biggest phone companies in America."

Tenzin's eyebrows flickered upward momentarily. "I hope he's improved his manners, or he won't be working there very long."

"I am sure his manners are much improved," said Lobsang, "now that he's escaped his own fear of failure."

He chuckled as he continued to read the card. "Just last week he repaired the telephone of this one." He held up the postcard.

"Who is she?" asked Chogyal.

"A very famous American actress who is also something of a patron saint of stray cats." He turned to look at me with a knowing expression that belied his claim not to have any special qualities.

"This postcard closes the circle on our meeting with Raj Goel very nicely, wouldn't you say, HHC?"

CHAPTER ELEVEN

Is there a downside to being the Dalai Lama's Cat?

Simply asking the question may seem preposterous or suggest such base ingratitude that you many want to dismiss me this instant as an overpampered wretch, one of those flat-faced, long-haired felines whose expression of icy hauteur gives the impression that nothing ever will be quite good enough for them.

But not so fast, dear reader. Are there not two sides to every story?

It's true that there can be few cats in history who have benefited from the peerless conditions in which I find myself. Not only are all my material needs fulfilled and my whims indulged—sometimes before I'm even aware of them myself—but my cerebral world is enlivened by the rich variety of visitors and activities that swirl around me. Emotionally, it would be hard to imagine being more loved, worshipped, and adored by those for whom I, in turn, have only the most heart-felt devotion.

And spiritually, as you already know, all it takes is for His Holiness to step into a room, and all ordinary appearances and conceptions seem to dissolve away, leaving only an abiding sensation of profound well-being. Given that I spend so much of each day in his presence, sleep through every night at the foot of his bed, and spend many hours in his lap, I must be one of the most blissed-out cats on the planet.

Where, pray tell, is the downside of all of that?

As the Dalai Lama frequently explains, inner development is something for which we must each take personal responsibility. Other beings cannot make us more mindful, so that we can experience the rich tapestry of everyday experience to the fullest. Similarly, other beings cannot force us to become more patient or kind, no matter how conducive to our contentment patience or kindness would be. As for improving concentration while meditating, this is, quite obviously, something we need to do for ourselves.

And so we come to the heart of the matter, the cause of my embarrassing but undeniable vexation.

Day after day, I sit in audiences with His Holiness, listening to the meditation experiences of advanced practitioners, knowing that I am incapable of meditating for more than two minutes without being distracted. Not a week goes by that I don't hear about amazing adventures in consciousness undertaken by yogis who are asleep or technically—if temporarily—dead. But when I close my own eyes each night, I quickly fall into a state of heavy, oblivious torpor.

If I lived with a family who spent as much time watching television as the Dalai Lama spends meditating, and whose minds were just as agitated as my own, perhaps then, I sometimes think, I wouldn't be quite so painfully aware of my own limitations. If I were surrounded by humans who believed that it is the people and things in their lives that make them happy or unhappy, rather than their attitude toward those people or things—well, then I could be considered the very wisest of cats.

But I'm not.

So I can't be.

Instead, there are times when I feel so inadequate it seems pointless to even try becoming a genuine bodhicatva. My poor meditation skills. My habitual negative mental thoughts. Living at Jokhang is like being a pygmy among giants! Not to mention the fact that I have all manner of personal inadequacies, like my shadow side of gluttonous craving, which I battle each and every day, and my physical imperfections, instantly evident when I begin to walk, on account of my wobbly hind legs. And the acutely painful knowledge, like a sharp-edged grain of sand chafing at the very heart of my self-esteem, that my impeccable breeding is—oh, woe upon woes!—undocumented and likely to remain so till the end of time. It's hard to keep believing that you are different or special or—dare one say it, blue-blooded—without the paperwork to prove it.

These were my precise thoughts when I ambled down the road one morning to Café Franc for a comfort meal. Making my way through the bustling tables,

I paused to exchange wet-nose greetings with Marcel, who had become more cordial toward me since the arrival of Kyi Kyi. I indulged Franc with a beneficent purr when he reached down to stroke me. Then, darting out of the way of the head waiter, Kusali, who was balancing three plates of food on each arm, I ascended to my usual place between the glossy fashion magazines and surveyed my private theater.

There was the usual mixture of travelers—hikers, Seekers, Greenies, and sneaker-clad retirees. But my attention was immediately drawn to the 30-something man sitting alone at the table directly beside me, reading a copy of Bruce Lipton's *The Biology of Belief.* Fresh-faced and handsome, with hazel eyes, a high forehead, and curly, dark hair, he was reading at a pace that suggested a ferocious intellect behind a pair of somewhat nerdy reading glasses.

Sam Goldberg was one of the longer-term patrons of the café. Arriving in McLeod Ganj a month earlier, on discovering Café Franc he had immediately become a daily visitor. It hadn't taken Franc long to introduce himself.

The two of them had exchanged the usual small talk, during which I learned that Sam was taking time off after being laid off from his job in Los Angeles. He was in McLeod Ganj for an indeterminate time. He read an average of four books a week. He was an inveterate blogger on mind/body/spirit matters. And he had an online following of over 20,000 people.

It was during a conversation the previous week, however, that an interesting new possibility had emerged. During a lull between the midmorning and lunchtime crowds, Franc had pulled up a chair opposite Sam—an honor he bestowed only rarely on customers.

"What are you reading today?" he asked, sliding a complimentary latte toward Sam.

"Oh, thank you! Very kind." Sam glanced at the coffee—and only very briefly at Franc—before returning his gaze to the book. "It's the Dalai Lama's commentary on the Heart Sutra," he said. "One of the classics and a personal favorite. I must have read it a dozen times. Along with Thich Naht Hanh's *Heart of Understanding*, I have found it the most useful work in helping unlock the sutra's meaning."

"Dependent arising is a difficult topic," remarked Franc.

"The most difficult," agreed Sam. "But for a broader understanding you can't go much beyond Tilopa's *Mahamudra Instruction to Naropa in Twenty-Eight Verses* or the First Panchen Lama's *Main Road of the Triumphant Ones*. Tilopa's verses are wonderfully lyrical, and poetry can sometimes convey a meaning that goes well beyond the words themselves. The Panchen Lama's teachings are much more prosaic. But their power and clarity are exactly what you need when meditating on such a subtle object."

Franc digested this in silence for a moment before saying, "It amazes me, Sam. Seems whatever subject I ask you about, you can rattle off the names of half a dozen books on the subject, together with a full critique."

"Oh, n-n-n-n-no." Flecks of pink appeared on Sam's pale neck.

"I suppose you have to keep up with things for your blog?"

"Actually, the blog was a result"—Sam flashed a quick glance toward Franc without actually making eye contact—"rather than the cause."

"You've always been a bookworm?"

"It helps if you are, in the industry. Th-th-the industry I used to be in, I mean."

"And what industry was that?" asked Franc conversationally.

"Bookselling."

"You mean . . . ?"

"I used to work for one of the chain bookstores."

"That's . . . intriguing." I recognized the gleam in Franc's eye. It was the same gleam I'd seen when he discovered I was the Dalai Lama's cat.

"I ran a mind/body/spirit section," continued Sam. "Needed to keep up to date with all the titles."

"Tell me," Franc said, leaning forward, elbows on the table. "This move to e-books and electronic readers. Does it mean the end of bookstores?"

Sam drew himself up in his chair before managing to look Franc in the eye for a full second. "Nobody has a crystal ball, but I think there are actually some stores that will thrive. Those that sell a particular kind of book. Perhaps organize events."

"Like book cafés?"

"Exactly."

Franc regarded Sam carefully for a long while before telling him, "For the past few months I've been wondering how I can diversify my business. I have that area, separate from the rest of the tables, that is under-utilized." He gestured toward the part of the café, up a few steps, where the lighting was more subdued and the tables often unoccupied. "I have a lot of tourists passing through here every day who may want to buy a new book—and there's nowhere locally to buy one. Problem is, I know nothing about running a bookstore. And I didn't know anyone who did, until now."

Sam nodded.

"So, what do you think of the idea?"

"This is exactly the kind of place I could see a bookstore doing well. Like you say, there is no competition. It doesn't hurt that mobile reception is hit-and-miss around these parts, making it hard to download e-books—"

"A lot of our customers already have a strong interest in mind/body/spirit books," interjected Franc. "They're in here reading them all the time."

"If they're coming for the overall experience," chimed in Sam, "you could broaden that experience to include buying new books, CDs, perhaps gifts."

"Buddhist and Indian novelty items."

"Only the better-quality stuff."

"Of course."

For a full three seconds, Sam held Franc's gaze. The gleam in Franc's eye had developed into full-blown excitement. Even Sam's customary shyness seemed to have lifted.

Then Franc asked, "Will you set it up for me?"

"You mean—?"

"And run it. As my bookstore manager."

The enthusiasm quickly drained from Sam's face.

"Well, that's v-v-very nice of you to ask, but I couldn't." Deep furrows appeared on his forehead between his eyes. "I mean, I'm only here for a few weeks."

"You've no job to go back to," Franc reminded him, somewhat brutally. "I'm offering you a job here."

"But my visa—"

Franc waved dismissively. "I've got a guy who can take care of the paperwork."

"And ac-c-c-commodation—"

"There's an apartment upstairs," said Franc. "I can make that part of the deal."

But instead of resolving Sam's concerns, Franc seemed only to be compounding them. Sam lowered his face as a red blush appeared, first on his neck, then steadily, inexorably, bloomed on his cheeks.

"I just couldn't do it," he told Franc. "Even if everything else was . . . "

Leaning forward in his chair, Franc eyeballed him. "Why not?"

Sam stared miserably at the floor.

"You can tell me," Franc said, softening his tone.

Sam shook his head slowly.

After a pause, Franc tried a different tack. "Trust me—I'm a Buddhist."

Sam smiled sadly.

"I'm not leaving here"—Franc managed to combine both sympathy and insistence in his tone—"until you tell me."

He sat back in his chair, as though preparing for a long wait. Sam's blush deepened a shade. Then, after the lengthiest pause, eyes still fixed to the floor, Sam murmured, "When the store in Century City closed, I was laid off."

"You said."

"Thing is, not everyone was laid off. A few were kept on and redeployed." Sam hung his head in shame.

"And you're thinking—?"

"If I'd been any good at my job, I would have been kept on, too."

"They kept the top performers, did they?" Franc's voice was tight. "What other reason? The cost of laying them off? Were they long-term employees?"

Sam shrugged. "I guess. Most of them. But you can see how . . . bad I am with people. I'd be no good at it, Franc." He finally managed the very briefest glance in Franc's direction. "At school, I was always the last kid left when the others picked sports teams. At college, I could never get a date. I'm just not a people person. I'd be a disaster."

As Franc regarded the pitiable figure in front of him, a knowing, impish expression played on his lips. Silently, he gestured to Kusali to bring him an espresso.

"Yeah, I agree," he responded after a while. "Imagine how disastrous it would be having someone who knew the category backward doing all our ordering. Or if customers asked you about a subject, and you offered them half a dozen alternatives. That could be catastrophic!"

"It's not that—"

"Say someone came in here wanting to pick a sports team and the first person they saw was you."

"You know I didn't mean—"

"Or, God help us, a single woman turned up on the prowl for a date!"

"It's about talking to people," Sam retorted, almost fiercely. "I'm no good at it."

"You talk to me."

"You're not a customer."

"I've never pressured anyone into ordering a cappuccino, and I wouldn't expect you to lay on the hard sell, if that's what you mean," said Franc.

The two of them looked at each other evenly before Franc said, "Either the bookstore idea is going to work, or it's not. I believe you're the right man for the job, even if you don't believe it yourself."

That conversation took place late last week, and despite Franc's best efforts, it had ended without Sam committing to anything. He had been in the café every day since, but nothing more on the subject was said. I wondered how long Franc would be able to hold off. Because I had no doubt he would be bringing up the subject again.

Since the conversation with Sam, Franc had called in several tradesmen to measure the space he was considering for a bookshop and to discuss shelving and display options. But could he get Sam to budge?

As it happened, Franc's powers of persuasion were irrelevant. Not long after I arrived that morning and found Sam engrossed on the subject of cellular biology and epigenetics, who should appear in the café but Geshe Wangpo.

As Franc had quickly discovered, having a teacher was a double-edged sword. The benefits were extraordinary, but so were the demands. And when your teacher was as uncompromising a lama as Geshe Wangpo, the edges of that sword were razor sharp. Every Tuesday evening, Franc attended classes on the Path to Enlightenment up at the temple, but at other moments, Geshe Wangpo would burst into his world unexpectedly, with life-changing results.

On one occasion, serious problems with his waitstaff had left Franc bamboozled and despairing. Geshe Wangpo phoned him, unprecedented and unprompted, ordering him, in the shortest of calls, to recite Green Tara mantras for two hours every day. By the end of that week, Franc's human resource problems had mysteriously resolved themselves.

On a different occasion, Franc had just put the phone down from talking to his father, who had made a long-distance call from his sickbed in San Francisco. Franc had spent the previous ten minutes explaining why he couldn't possibly go home to visit when he turned and discovered his lama standing right behind him. Geshe Wangpo had ordered him, in no uncertain terms, to make visiting his father a priority. What sort of son did he think he was, telling a frail and elderly old man that he was too busy to see him? Who did he think he owed his life to? What kind of parents did he want in future lifetimes—those as offhanded and disregarding as Franc was planning to be, or parents who would genuinely care about his well-being? And, by the way, he should make sure to buy his father good-quality gifts from Duty Free.

Half an hour later, Franc had booked his ticket home.

Today, when Geshe Wangpo arrived at the café during the midmorning lull, he glanced around at the sea of unoccupied tables before making his way directly toward where Sam Goldberg sat alone reading. There was a powerful energy in the way he moved across the room, as though he weren't a maroon-clad monk making an appearance but an altogether more commanding being—a large, blue-black, fire-breathing monster like the ones portrayed in the temple thangkas, perhaps.

"May I sit here?" he asked, pulling out the chair opposite Sam.

"Y-yes. Sure." Almost all of the tables around them were unoccupied, but if Sam found the request strange, he betrayed no sign of it. Instead, he returned to his book.

Having made himself comfortable, Geshe Wangpo had no intention of keeping to himself. "What are you reading?"

Sam looked up. "A book on, er, epigenetics."

The lama glanced at three paperbacks stacked beside Sam's empty coffee cup. "You like to read?"

Sam nodded.

I wondered if Franc had spoken to Geshe Wangpo about his bookstore idea after class that week, but it seemed unlikely. Geshe Wangpo encouraged self-sufficiency in his students. As for Sam, he had no idea who Geshe Wangpo was, apart from an unusually forward monk.

"It is *most* useful," Geshe Wangpo told Sam, "to share one's knowledge with others. Otherwise, what is the point in having it?"

Sam looked up at the lama—and held his eye. This was not his usual darting glance but contact that continued for an improbable length of time. What was it in the lama's face that held his gaze? Was it something that reassured him, perhaps, conveying a sense of the safety and profound compassion that resided beneath the Tibetan's stern exterior? Was Geshe Wangpo holding Sam's gaze simply through the force of personality for which he was well known? Or was a different connection being made—one less easy to explain?

Whichever it was, when Sam finally replied, it was without any of his customary shyness. "Strange that you should say that. The owner here asked if I would run a bookstore for him." He gestured toward the unused area Franc had in mind.

"Do you want to?" asked the lama.

Sam grimaced. "I don't think I'd be any good at it."

Geshe Wangpo's expression was unchanged. He tried again. "Do you want to?"

"I couldn't let him down. He'd have to invest a lot of money in stock and display units. If it all went wrong because of me . . . "

"I hear, I hear." Geshe Wangpo leaned forward. "But do you want to?"

A small, rueful, but irresistible smile appeared at the corners of Sam's mouth.

Before he could say a word, Geshe Wangpo told him, "Then you must do it!"

Sam's smile broadened. "I have been thinking about it. A lot. It could be a . . . stimulating fresh start. But I have reservations."

"What are 'reservations'?" The lama's eyebrows crinkled theatrically.

"Reservations?" Sam consulted the thesaurus in his mind. "Doubts. Concerns. Uncertainties."

"That is normal," the other told him. Then, to emphasize, he said it again, deeper, louder, and slower: "Normal."

"I was analyzing the opportunity—" Sam started to explain.

But Geshe Wangpo cut him short. "Too much thinking is not necessary."

Sam stared at him, taken aback to hear cognitive inquiry so casually dismissed. "You haven't seen me with people," he continued. "Ordinary people."

Hands on his hips, the lama sat forward in his seat. "There is a problem?"

Sam shrugged. "You could probably say a self-esteem issue."

"Self-esteem?"

"When you don't think you're up to it."

Geshe Wangpo was unconvinced. "But you read many books. You have the knowledge."

"It's not that."

"In Buddhism"—the lama tilted his head back challengingly—"we would say that you are lazy."

Sam's reaction was the opposite of his usual. Color drained from his face.

"Despising yourself, thinking you are no good, saying 'I can't do this.' This is the mind of weakness. You must work to overcome it."

"It's not through choice," Sam protested faintly.

"Then you must *choose* to overcome. What happens if you keep giving in to a weak mind? You feed weakness. The result is an even weaker mind in the future. Instead, you must cultivate confidence!" Geshe Wangpo sat erect in his chair and clenched his fist on the table. Power seemed to emanate from him in all directions.

"You think I can?"

"You must!" the lama told him forcefully. "When you talk to people, you must speak to them with big eyes and a strong voice."

Sam was shifting to a straighter posture in his chair.

"You have read *A Guide to the Bodhisattva's Way of Life*?"

Sam was nodding.

"It says self-confidence should be applied to wholesome actions. That is what you would do here, yes— wholesome actions? You must decide 'I alone shall do it.' This is the self-confidence of action."

"Big eyes and a strong voice?" Sam asked, noticeably louder.

The lama nodded. "Like this."

In response to Geshe Wangpo's power, a new feeling seemed to be coming over Sam. He was sitting more upright. Holding himself more assertively. Instead of staring downward, he looked directly into Geshe Wangpo's eyes. Nothing was being said out loud, but in the silence a different, more intuitive form of communication seemed to be occurring. As though Sam were realizing that all his self-esteem issues were nothing more than ideas he had about himself, ideas that had all the substance of tissue paper. Ideas that were temporary and, like any other, would arise, abide, and pass. Ideas that, in the presence of this monk, were being replaced by different, more life-affirming ones.

He spoke after the longest while. "I don't know your name," he said.

"Geshe Acharya Trijang Wangpo."

"Not the author of *Path to the Union of No More Learning,* translated by Stephanie Spinster?"

The lama sat back in his chair, folded his arms across his chest, and threw Sam a look of glowering challenge. "You know plenty," he said.

As I padded back to Jokhang later that day, I was lost in my own thoughts about what Geshe Wangpo had said. I'd been as startled as Sam to hear that a lack of self-confidence was considered, in Buddhism, to be a form of laziness, a weak mind that had to be overcome. I couldn't avoid remembering my own feelings of inadequacy when it came to Dharma practice in general and meditation in particular. And how, living at

Jokhang and being frequently reminded of the transcendent realizations that were possible, my own meditation practice was so limited that it seemed hardly worth continuing.

But as Franc's lama had said, what would happen if I kept giving in to a weak mind? What result could there possibly be except future weakness? There was an unavoidable, if disconcerting logic, but along with it, a strangely compelling feeling of empowerment.

That evening, as I took up my meditation position on the windowsill, my paws neatly tucked beneath me, eyes half-closed and whiskers alert, before I focused on my breathing, I recalled Geshe Wangpo's words.

I reminded myself that I lived with the perfect role model, that I was surrounded by those who supported my practice. There were no better circumstances than mine in which to evolve into a true bodhicatva.

I alone must do this!

Did I arise from that meditation session as a fully enlightened being? Was my change of attitude the cause of instant nirvana? Dear reader, I would be lying if I told you so. My meditation showed no sign of instant improvement, but perhaps more importantly, my feelings about it did.

Starting then, I decided that I wasn't going to think of every bad session as a reason to give up. I wouldn't judge my own experience according to the Olympian heights achieved by His Holiness's visitors. I was HHC, with my own failings and weaknesses, but, like Sam, my own strengths, too. I would meditate, metaphorically speaking, with big eyes and a strong voice. I might not have all the instructions about meditative concentration down pat, but I knew plenty.

There is a postscript to this story, dear reader. Of course there is—that's the best bit, don't you think? The unexpected bonbon. The balletic pirouette. When it comes to sudden shifts in gear, I am that kind of cat.

This is just such a book.

And, having come this far with me, like it or not, my friend, you are most certainly that type of reader!

First, a confession.

I had been unsettled the day I had listened to Sam's spiraling self-doubt, as he explained his feelings of inadequacy to Franc. How being laid off from the bookstore had underlined the rejection he had felt at being the last boy standing at sports-team selections. How his failure to find love at college only reinforced the saga of a woeful misfit. The fact that many highly capable professionals had no sporting prowess, or that some of the most gorgeous women happily partnered with the geekiest of men, somehow didn't deflect his self-destructive beliefs. Considering how intelligent he was, his explanation was bizarre and would even have been laughable were it not for the pain it so obviously caused him.

And yet when I had listened to how he combined an assortment of disconnected experiences to produce an elaborately depressing narrative about himself, I couldn't avoid a painful recognition: I was just like that.

Didn't I allow one negative thought to spark off a quite unrelated one? No sooner was I reflecting on my poor meditation skills than I would turn to my lack of discipline at the food bowl. Contemplating my physical form, I'd dwell on the absurd way I walked because of the injury to my legs. Which led, with depressing inevitability, to my earliest memories and the matter of my pedigree.

After the jolt delivered by Geshe Wangpo, I came to discover the opposite dynamic: that positive thoughts also multiply—and produce the most unexpectedly wonderful effects.

There is a quotation attributed to Goethe, much loved by the manufacturers of fridge magnets, greeting cards, and other inspirational trinkets. It runs: "Whatever you can do or dream you can, begin it. Boldness has genius, power, and magic in it." Although Tenzin told me that Goethe never wrote any such thing, the words have a compelling resonance to them.

Once I began to be more self-confident about my meditation practice, I found it affected a lot of other things. I wouldn't eat every last scrap of Mrs. Trinci's diced chicken liver just because it was there. I would walk, tail high, into meetings with the most distinguished of His Holiness's visitors. Why shouldn't I?

And the most curious of things: Tashi and Sashi, the street-urchins-turned-novices whom His Holiness had instructed to take particular care of me, continued to visit me in the Jokhang visitors' room from time to time. Usually they'd sit on the floor for five minutes and scratch my neck. Sometimes they'd recite mantras.

One afternoon, a few days after my change in attitude, they happened to visit. Following the usual format, I rolled onto an elaborate rug, arms and legs splayed, to allow them to run their fingers up and down my tummy.

It was at this point that Chogyal came into the room.

"Very nice." He nodded to the two boys with a smile.

"She has grown into a beautiful cat," said Tashi.

"A Himalayan," Chogyal told them, bending to massage the velvety tips of my ears. "Usually, only wealthy people can afford cats such as this one."

Sashi had a faraway look in his eye for a while before he said, "This cat's mother was owned by wealthy people."

"She was?" Chogyal raised his eyebrows.

"Even though we were in a poor area, we used to watch the mother walk along the wall from the big house—"

"Very big house," interjected Tashi. "With *its own swimming pool!*"

"She went there to eat," Sashi said.

"One day we followed her to the kittens—" Tashi began.

"That's how we found them," finished Sashi.

"They had several very shiny Mercedes at that house," Tashi recalled. "And a servant whose only job was to keep them polished!"

Chogyal straightened. "How interesting. It seems that HHC may be a purebreed after all. But you know, it is our vow, as Buddhists, not to take anything unless it is freely given. I wonder if it is possible to contact the family she originally came from, to offer them payment."

CHAPTER TWELVE

Visits by heads of state almost always created a stir of activity at Jokhang. In the days running up to them, hatchet-faced intelligence officers would want to see the inside of every cupboard in the complex. Chiefs of protocol would meet to discuss the tiniest of details. Extraordinary lengths were taken to ensure that every contingency was accounted for, from the location of security detachments on nearby rooftops to the texture of toilet paper provided for the VIPs, should that particular need arise.

This was why I was caught completely unaware the day His Holiness received a visitor who was not just a national leader but a real-life queen.

There had been none of the usual elaborate preparation beforehand. Only a low-key security visit half an hour earlier, which was ironic, because I knew that this particular royal visitor was one whom His Holiness was especially eager to meet. I had overheard him speak of both the young queen and her husband very warmly in the past. Not only was she extraordinarily beautiful but she was married to the king of the only Himalayan Buddhist country in the world.

I am talking, of course, about the queen of Bhutan.

For those readers who didn't spend their school days poring over atlases of the Himalaya region—do such people exist?—Bhutan is a small country east of Nepal, south of Tibet, and a bit north of Bangladesh. It's the kind of place that might have escaped your attention had a flake of smoked salmon fallen from your bagel onto just the wrong spot on the map. The same point could be made about half the countries in Europe, but to have missed Bhutan would be a terrible oversight, because it is, quite simply, the closest place to Shangri-la on Earth.

A remote and secluded kingdom, impenetrable behind the Himalaya ranges, until the 1960s Bhutan had no national currency or telephones, and television only arrived in 1999. The focus of people's lives has traditionally been on cultivating inner wealth rather than material well-being. It was the ruling King of Bhutan himself who, in the 1980s, set up a system that measured national advancement according to Gross National Happiness rather than Gross Domestic Product.

A land of gold-roofed temples perched on the unlikeliest cliff ledges, of prayer flags fluttering across deep, mountain chasms, and of monks chanting in incense-suffused seventh-century temples, Bhutan is pervaded by a magical quality. And there was an extraordinary presence to the young queen when she appeared in His Holiness's suite.

I had been at my usual place on the windowsill, dozing in the morning sun, when I heard her announced by Lobsang. At the words "Her Royal Highness," I rolled onto my back and let my head hang over the edge of the sill.

Even viewing her upside down, I could see she was the most exquisite of beings. Petite, golden-skinned, with long hair that was dark and lustrous, she had a captivating delicacy about her. In her traditional Bhutanese *kira*—an ornately embroidered ankle-length dress—she seemed almost doll-like. Yet the way she moved was natural and unaffected, suggesting great personal warmth.

I watched her present His Holiness with the traditional white scarf, her face bowed and hands folded together at her heart in a gesture of devotion. After the ceremonial exchange she glanced around the room before sitting down—and immediately caught sight of me.

Our eyes met and even though we held each other's gaze for the briefest of moments, something important was communicated. I instantly knew that she was one of us.

A cat lover.

When she sat down, it seemed to me that she brushed her kira flat on her lap in anticipation of what would happen next. Rolling off the sill, I landed on the carpet and performed a sun salutation, luxuriantly stretching out my front paws, then a reverse sun salutation, tremulously shuddering my hind quarters with a shimmy of my tail, before making my way to where she sat. Hopping up onto her lap, I settled immediately, and she began stroking my neck, like the old friends we intuitively knew we were.

There is a rare minority of humans who possess an innate understanding of the changing moods of a cat: how what we might want at one moment may be quite different from what we wished for only moments before. Some people know that they should not keep stroking a cat until we are forced to turn around and deliver a sharp, incisive warning—usually focused on the index finger. A small proportion understand that just because we wolfed down a can of grilled turkey with lip-smacking relish one day it does not mean we have the slightest interest in even looking at the same food the next.

Was it not Winston Churchill who said that a cat is a riddle, inside an enigma, inside a delightful pelt of cuddliness? No? I could have sworn that just recently I read something to that effect in an article about him. And if he didn't say it, he almost certainly thought it. Wikipedia should be told!

And then there's Albert Einstein, who reportedly said that music and cats offer the only escape from the miseries of life. Note that on the subject of other species of domesticated animals, the greatest thinker of the 20th century remained curiously mute. I will leave it to you, dear reader, to draw your own conclusions.

We cats are not robotic beasts who can be conditioned to jump up or sit down or salivate at the utterance of a command or the press of a bell. Did you ever hear of Pavlov's *cat?*

My point exactly. The very thought is unimaginable!

No, cats are indeed a mystery, sometimes even to ourselves. Most people are willing to treat us with the respect accorded to those who add so much to the sum of human contentment while making so few demands. Only a rare few truly understand us. And the queen of Bhutan is among that elite minority.

After a few getting-to-know-you strokes, she drew her fingertips together and massaged my forehead with her nails, sending shivers of exquisite pleasure all the way down my spine to the tingling tip of my tail.

I rewarded her with a deep-throated purr.

His Holiness, who had been making polite inquiries about the health of the king and other Bhutanese royals, looked over at me. It was his habit to ask visitors if they minded having me in the room. Some humans, it seems, are afflicted with an allergy that must be as devastating as a violent reaction to, say, Belgian truffles, Italian coffee, or Mozart. The queen was being so attentive to me that the Dalai Lama had no need to ask, but nodding in my direction, he did say, "This is quite exceptional. I have never known her to take to someone so quickly! She must like you very much."

"And I like her," Her Royal Highness replied. "She is magnificent!"

"Our little Snow Lion."

"I'm sure she brings you much enjoyment." The queen moved her fingertips to massage my charcoal ears with just the right degree of firmness.

His Holiness chuckled. "She has a great personality!"

Conversation moved on; the queen discussing various Dharma practices. As they talked, she continued her delightful ministrations, and I was soon in a state of semiconscious bliss, with the conversation between the two of them passing above me.

In recent weeks I had been making a conscientious effort with my own daily meditations, after the stern wake-up call delivered by Geshe Wangpo. I had also taken myself off to the temple a number of times, attending the teachings of a variety of high-ranking lamas. Every time, a different aspect of Dharma practice was discussed. And on each occasion, the practice seemed very important.

Mind training is the foundation of all Buddhist activities, and we are encouraged to develop strong concentration not only when meditating but also by practicing mindfulness throughout each day. As one of the lamas explained, if we are not objectively aware of our thoughts moment by moment and instead engage with every one of them, how can we begin to change them? "You can't manage what you don't monitor," he said. Mindfulness, it seems, is a foundation practice.

A different teacher explained how the six perfections are the very heart of our tradition. If we fail to practice generosity, ethics, and patience, to name just three, what is the point of learning texts or reciting mantras? Without virtue, the teacher said, none of our other Dharma activities would be very meaningful.

Yet another lama explained how wisdom about the nature of reality is what distinguishes Buddha's teachings from all others. The way the world appears to us is illusory, he emphasized, and understanding this very subtle truth requires a great deal of listening, thinking, and meditation. Only those who understand the truth directly and nonconceptually can achieve nirvana.

As my thoughts continued to weave in and out of the conversation between the queen and the Dalai

Lama, I remembered the teaching I had been to only the previous night. There in the soft-lit temple, with innumerable buddhas and bodhisattvas looking down on us in the form of statues and wall hangings, one of Namgyal Monastery's most revered yogis had described the rich esoteric tradition of tantra practices, including those focused on White Tara and Medicine Buddha. Each of the practices came with its own text, or *sadhana*, to recite, along with visualizations and accompanying mantras. Certain tantras are of vital importance, the yogi explained, if we wish to attain enlightenment quickly.

Who doesn't?

The more I was learning about Tibetan Buddhism, the more I realized how very little I knew. No question, the teachings were stimulating and engaging, and there was always some new and intriguing practice around the corner. But I was also feeling confused.

Only half aware of the conversation continuing above me, I returned to full consciousness when I heard the queen say, "Your Holiness, there are so many different practices in our tradition. But which of them is the most important?"

It was as if she had been reading my mind! That was *my* question, though I hadn't put it in so many words. It was what I too wanted to know!

His Holiness did not hesitate. "Without question, the most important practice is *bodhichitta*."

"The wish to attain enlightenment in order to lead all living beings to that same state," she confirmed.

He nodded. "This mind of enlightenment is based on pure, great compassion, which in turn is founded on pure, great love. In each case *pure* means impartial.

Without conditions. And *great* means benefiting all living beings, not just the small group of those we happen to like at the moment.

"From our perspective, the only way to enjoy a state of permanent happiness and avoid all suffering is to achieve enlightenment. This is why bodhichitta is considered to be the most altruistic of motivations. We wish to achieve enlightenment not only for ourselves but to help every other living being reach the same state."

"A very challenging motivation."

His Holiness smiled. "Of course! It is a lifetime's task to turn the mind of enlightenment from just a nice idea into sincere conviction. When we begin, it can feel as if we're only acting. We may think, *Who am I fooling, trying to pretend I can become a buddha and lead all living beings to enlightenment?* But step by step, we develop understanding. We find that others have done it already. We develop confidence in our own capabilities. We learn to become less self-focused and more other-focused.

"I once heard an interesting definition of a holy person: 'A holy person is someone who thinks more of others than of themselves.' This is useful, don't you agree?"

Her Royal Highness nodded before musing, "Agreeing with the idea of bodhichitta is one thing. But remembering to put it into practice . . . "

"Yes, being mindful of bodhichitta is most useful. We can apply it to so many of our actions of body, speech, and mind. Our everyday life is rich with possibilities to practice bodhichitta—and each time we do, as Buddha said, the positive impact on our mind is beyond measure."

"Why so great, Your Holiness?"

The Dalai Lama leaned forward in his chair. "The power of virtue is much, much stronger than the power of negativity. And there is no greater virtue than bodhichitta. When we cultivate this mind we are focusing on inner qualities, not external ones. We are recollecting the well-being of others, not thinking only of the self. This is, you see, a panoramic perspective, not limited to the short-term future of this life. It goes against all our usual thoughts. We are setting our minds on a very different, very powerful trajectory."

"You said that every day life is rich with possibilities to practice?"

His Holiness nodded. "Every time we do something nice for someone else, even if it is a routine thing they expect, we can do so with the thought 'By this act of love, or of giving happiness, may I attain enlightenment to liberate all living beings.' Every time we practice generosity, whether it is making a donation or nursing a cat, we can think the same thing."

At that moment I yawned deeply. The Dalai Lama and the queen both laughed.

Then, as she looked down into my sapphire eyes, Her Royal Highness said, "It's karma, isn't it, that brings people and other beings into our lives?"

His Holiness nodded. "If there is a very strong connection, sometimes the same being can come back again and again."

"Some people think it is silly to practice mantra recitation aloud for the benefit of animals."

"No, not silly," said His Holiness. "This can be very useful. We can create—how do you say?—a good karmic imprint on the mental continuum of a being that can ripen when it meets the right conditions in the future. There are stories in the scriptures of how meditators said mantras out loud to birds. In future lives, the birds were drawn to the Dharma and were able to find enlightenment."

"So little Snow Lion must have some very, very good karmic imprints?"

The Dalai Lama beamed. "Undoubtedly!"

It was then that the queen said something that seemed most unusual. More unusual still, with the benefit of hindsight. "If she ever has kittens of her own," she murmured, "it would be my very great honor to give one of them a home."

His Holiness clapped his hands together. "Very good!" he said.

"I mean it!"

The Dalai Lama met her eyes with an expression of oceanic benevolence. "I will remember," he said.

A few mornings later I sashayed into the executive assistants' office. The phones were quiet, the day's mail had yet to arrive, and during the unusual lull in activity, Chogyal had made cups of tea, which the two men were enjoying with several pieces of Scottish shortbread, courtesy of Mrs. Trinci.

"Good morning, HHC," Chogyal greeted, as I rubbed my body against his robe-clad legs. He leaned down to stroke me.

Tenzin leaned back in his chair. "How long has she been with us, would you say?"

Chogyal shrugged. "A year?"

"Longer than that."

"It was before Kyi Kyi."

"*Way* before Kyi Kyi." Tenzin bit into his sugar-dusted shortbread with diplomatic finesse. "Wasn't it around the time of the visit from that Oxford professor?"

"I can tell you exactly." Chogyal leaned forward to his computer and called up a calendar. "Remember? It was the day His Holiness got back from an American trip."

"That's right!"

"Which was thirteen, fourteen . . . sixteen months ago."

"That long?"

"Impermanence," Chogyal reminded him, snapping his fingers.

"Hmm."

"Is there any reason—?"

"I was just thinking," Tenzin said, "she's no longer a kitten. When she had her vaccinations, they suggested we take her in to have her spayed. And a microchip implant."

"I'll make a note to contact the vet," Chogyal said, adding this to his daily To Do list. "Friday afternoon I should have some time to take her in."

That Friday afternoon found me sitting on Chogyal's lap in the back of the Dalai Lama's car as the driver—the less said about him the better—drove us from Jokhang to the modern veterinary surgery in Dharamsala. There was no need for cages, hampers, or uncivilized yowling. I am, after all, His Holiness's Cat. On the way down the hill, I took a keen interest in the unfolding tableau, whiskers twitching with curiosity. If anything, it was

Chogyal who required soothing, as he held onto me nervously, muttering mantras under his breath.

Dr. Wilkinson, the tall, rangy Australian vet, soon had me on the examination table, where he proceeded to open my mouth, shine light beams in my ears, and subject me to the indignity of a temperature check.

"Time seems to have gotten away from us," Chogyal told him. "She's been with us for longer than we realized."

"She had her initial jabs," the vet reassured him. "That's the main thing. Lost a bit of weight since the last time I saw her, which she needed to do. Coat is in excellent condition."

"We'd like to have her microchipped. And spayed."

"Microchip"—Dr. Wilkinson was massaging my body—"always a good idea. We have people bring in lost pets all the time, and we have no way of contacting their owners. Heartbreaking."

He paused, hands no longer moving. "But we'll have to hold off the spaying for a while."

Chogyal's brow furrowed. "We weren't thinking now—"

"Six weeks. Maybe a month." The vet gave him a meaningful look.

Chogyal still wasn't getting it. "You're fully booked for operations?"

Dr. Wilkinson shook his head with a smile. "It's a bit late for spaying, mate," he told Chogyal. "His Holiness's Cat is to be a mother."

"What will we call them?" was the Driver's reaction when Chogyal broke the news on the way home.

Chogyal shrugged. I expect he had other things on his mind. Like how to break the news to His Holiness.

"Micey-Tungs?" suggested the driver.

EPILOGUE

Things were happening down at Café Franc. Sign painters had been up ladders for days, working on the façade of the restaurant. The area Franc was considering for a bookstore had been screened off. Judging from the muffled sounds of drilling and nailing, and the flurry of workmen in and out, all kinds of changes were taking place behind the floor-to-ceiling panels.

To anyone who asked, Franc explained that Café Franc was about to have "a major relaunch." It would be everything it had been in the past—but better. There would be more for customers and a wider variety of products. It would be an even nicer place to spend your time.

But exactly what was going on behind the scenes remained veiled in mystery.

This was an apt metaphor for my life right now. I was to become the mother of kittens. The changes in my body were rapid and significant. But exactly what this would mean to me was something I could only guess at. Exactly how many kittens would I have? In what way would they alter our life at Jokhang? Would they emerge as Himalayan, tabby, or somewhere in between?

One thing I knew for certain was that I had the Dalai Lama's full support. Following our visit to the vet, when Chogyal reported the news, His Holiness's face lit up. "Oh . . . how extraordinary!" His expression had been almost childlike with wonder as he leaned over to stroke me. "A litter of Snow Lion cubs. That will be fun!"

The question of my own origins, a riddle I believed would remain forever unsolved, was another area in which there had been sudden and unexpected change. Within days of Tashi and Sashi blurting out my origins, Chogyal had arranged for them to accompany him on his next visit to Delhi, to identify the family to whom my mother had belonged. They found the house without difficulty, but it was locked and guarded by a private security detail. There was no sign that a family was currently living there. No evidence at all of a feline in residence. A note had been left with one of the security guards, but a reply was yet to be forthcoming.

For all kinds of reasons, I felt I was living on the cusp of profound change. The tectonic plates of life were shifting. Things would never be the same again. I sensed the excitement of it, as well as the apprehension. But with the image of Geshe Wangpo vivid in my mind, I had all I needed. I was going to make this a positive transformation. I wasn't going to avoid any of it.

In particular, I wasn't going to miss out on the relaunch of Café Franc, which had been the cause of so much activity.

The event was scheduled for 6 P.M. one evening, but I made my way down the hill well in advance. My viewing platform was unaffected by the changes, which were no longer concealed by security screens but by large sheets of paper held together with a broad, red ribbon.

A crowd of people started trickling in as the time drew near. There were the McLeod Ganj regulars, always an eclectic mix, including people I knew from Jokhang. Mrs. Trinci arrived, fresh from the hairdresser, where she'd had her dark hair specially coiffed in honor of the occasion. Wearing a black dress, gold jewelry, and kohl eyes, she had added to her characteristic drama a certain Continental je ne sais quoi.

Chogyal also made an appearance in his capacity as Kyi Kyi's former guardian. Franc had soon led him over to show him the basket under the counter where both Kyi Kyi and Marcel, immaculate from the dog wash, wore red-and-gold bows around their necks.

As the drinks flowed freely and canapés circulated, the noise in the room grew ever louder. In the crowd I spotted Mrs. Patel from Cut Price Bazaar; these days, she greeted me, plateless and somewhat mournfully, whenever I passed her shop.

Sam was also there, positively debonair in a dark blue shirt and white linen sports jacket. In recent weeks he'd been a constant presence in the restaurant, as he and Franc managed the frenetic activity going on behind the screens. Since accepting Franc's offer, he had made a real effort to reinvent himself. Taking charge of the bookstore, he had summoned a succession of publishers' sales reps, had been quite clear about how point-of-sales gifts were to be displayed, and had directed tradesmen with newfound assertiveness. I had even seen him jab his hand emphatically at a carpenter whose workmanship hadn't been up to scratch.

Tenzin was in the crowd—a diplomatic presence talking to a pair of visiting academics from Harvard. Geshe Wangpo was standing at the front of the room near the ribbon, in a circle of senior Namgyal monks.

Franc was in his element, circulating throughout the room. But, unusually, today he had a very attractive, 30-something woman on his arm.

The metamorphosis of Franc had continued since that first encounter with Geshe Wangpo, reinforced by his visits to the classes at the temple every week. The golden Om earring and blessing strings had long since gone, the ascetically bald head now sported a surprisingly thick thatch of fair hair, and the clothes were less tight. And less black.

The biggest change was not visible. Gone was the hectoring bully who made life hell for the kitchen and waitstaff. There was no covering over his bursts of impatience, but instead of building to a frenzy of righteous indignation, now he seemed embarrassed when they happened. Gone, too, were the constant references to Dalai Lama this and Dharma that. The origins of Rinpoche were no longer mentioned, and I hadn't heard him even say the word Buddhist for weeks.

But exactly who was the young woman by his side? She had been in the café twice this week. The first time, she and Franc had spent more than two hours in earnest discussion at one of the pavement tables. The second time, he had taken her into the kitchen, where she'd spent a long time talking to the Dragpa brothers, as well as to Kusali.

Tonight she was resplendent in a coral red dress, long, dark hair swept straight down her back and jewelry glittering at her ears, throat, and wrists. I thought her the most exquisite woman I'd ever seen—there was such energy, such compassion in her features. As Franc introduced her to people, they seemed almost to melt in her presence, she conveyed such warmth.

Resting on my lotus cushion between *Vogue* and *Vanity Fair*, aware of the occasional movement in my distended belly, I looked out at the gathering crowd with a feeling of deep contentment for this moment, now, and all that had led me to it.

Kyi Kyi, lying in his basket under the counter, had arrived in my life at the same time as the self-development guru Jack. Through them I had come to understand the foolishness of being jealous of others' apparently wonderful lives, and to see that the true cause of happiness is the sincere wish to give happiness to others and help free them of all forms of dissatisfaction—love and compassion defined.

From Mrs. Trinci I had discovered that simply knowing these things was of little value. Our awareness of a truth needs to deepen to the point at which it actually changes our behavior. We call that a *realization*.

From the many people around me who practiced mindfulness, I realized how essential it is to attend to the present moment if we are to experience the rich variety of everyday life. Only by being fully awake to the present are we able to put our realizations into action— not to mention make every cup of coffee count.

Franc had been my teacher on fur balls—the danger of thinking about me, myself, and I to the point of becoming sick of myself. It was also because of him that I had discovered that the Dharma isn't about mouthing high-sounding principles, dressing in attention-seeking clothes, or calling yourself a Buddhist, but about expressing the teachings in your every thought, word, and deed.

And while the enormity of trying to become a more enlightened being might seem daunting at times, as Geshe Wangpo had explained, there is no room for laziness or a lack of confidence. Leading an authentic life calls for big eyes and a strong voice!

There was one guest notable for his absence on this occasion. The Dalai Lama was on his way back from the airport, after a brief trip overseas. Nonetheless, his presence was palpable, abiding with every one of us in the room, along with his message, "My religion is kindness." As Tibetan Buddhists, our central purpose is bodhichitta, arising out of a compassion to help all living beings find happiness.

People continued to arrive at Café Franc—I'd never seen the place so full. It was reaching the point of standing room only when Franc made his way to the front and onto a small platform set up for the dedication ceremony.

Someone tapped a glass loudly, and the hubbub in the room quickly diminished to a hush.

"Thanks to every one of you for coming," Franc said, glancing around at the assembled faces. "This is a very special day for all of us in the café community. And I have not just one announcement but three.

"The first is that because my father's health has taken a turn for the worse, I am leaving Café Franc to look after him."

There were gasps of sympathy and surprise.

"I could be in San Francisco for six to twelve months."

Geshe Wangpo, I noticed, was nodding approvingly.

"When I first realized I'd have to go, I wondered what to do about the café. I didn't want to have to close it down"—dismay rippled audibly through the audience—"but I knew it couldn't run on its own. Then, just two weeks ago, it was my amazing good fortune to meet

Serena Trinci, fresh from managing some of the finest restaurants in Europe." He gestured toward the young woman in red who he had been introducing all evening. She smiled broadly in acknowledgment.

"Serena has managed a two-Michelin-star restaurant in Bruges, the Hotel Danieli in Venice, and just recently was running one of the smartest society brasseries in London. But she couldn't avoid the call home to McLeod Ganj, and I'm delighted to tell you that she has kindly agreed to be caretaker while I'm away."

The announcement was greeted with a round of enthusiastic applause and a bow of appreciation from Serena. Mrs. Trinci looked on, glowing with maternal pride.

"For a long while I've been wondering how best to use the space behind here," Franc said, gesturing to the concealed area behind him. "I've had a few ideas but didn't know how to implement them. And then, in another spooky 'coincidence,' just the right person showed up at the right time." He nodded toward Sam, who was standing nearby.

"What I'd like to do now is ask my teacher and honored guest, Geshe Wangpo, to formally unveil our new addition."

Amid a smattering of applause, Geshe Wangpo joined Franc on the platform and walked over to the large, red bow. He was about to untie it before he remembered something. "Oh, yes. I am pleased to announce the opening of this marvelous new bookshop," he said, his hesitation prompting amusement. "May its existence be a cause for all living beings to have happiness and to avoid suffering."

As he tugged the ribbon, the panels of paper fell open, revealing gleaming rows of books, racks of CDs, and a colorful assortment of gifts. There was a wave of excited whooping and applause. Franc smiled as Geshe Wangpo gestured for Sam to join them on the podium. Sam vigorously shook his head, but Geshe Wangpo continued to insist. As Sam came to stand between the two men, the applause grew even louder, until the lama held up his hand in authoritative command.

"The books in this shop," he said, indicating the titles ranged in front of them, "are most useful. I know, because I have checked up. I think in future weeks there will be many monks from Namgyal Monastery visiting. They may not have money to buy, but they will check up."

Geshe Wangpo's straight-faced delivery prompted great mirth.

"The person choosing the books, this one"—he turned and gripped Sam by the arm—"has read *many* books. More than some lamas I know. He has great knowledge, but he is a little bit shy." There was a spark of mischief in the lama's eyes. "So you must be patient with him."

Far from looking down in embarrassment, Sam seemed energized by Geshe Wangpo's remarks. Returning the lama's smile, he looked out at the gathering and in a loud voice said, "We have a w-wonderful selection of book titles right here. All the old classics as well as some brand new releases. I can c-confidently say that this is a better stocked mind/body/spirit section than you'll find in even the bigger American bookstores. I look forward to seeing you all sometime soon."

A round of applause followed Sam's remarks. Beside him, Geshe Wangpo gave a cryptic smile.

"I'm sure you're all keen to get into the new section"—Franc took the lead again—"where you'll be pleased to know we do take credit cards. But before that I have our third announcement. Which is that effective immediately, Café Franc is to be renamed The Himalaya Book Café. We have a new sign out in front, unveiled tonight for the first time."

Another round of prolonged applause.

"When I first set up a business here, it was all about food and, I won't try to deny, all about me. I'm glad to say that things have changed since then. We're now about a lot more than just food. And fortunately we have grown way beyond just me. It is my very great privilege to work with the team of people here—Jigme and Ngawang Dragpa in the kitchen, Kusali and his team out front, and now Sam and Serena.

"So please, everyone, enjoy the food and drinks! Spend big on books and gifts! I look forward to seeing you all again when I am back from San Francisco!"

The launch party moved into full swing. No sooner was Sam in the bookstore than a line of eager purchasers formed at the till. In the restaurant, Franc circulated with Serena as the waitstaff replenished champagne and wine. The restaurant, now emporium, had never been so alive with energy, laughter, and joie de vivre.

How different all this was from the first time I'd visited Café Franc and was almost hurled forcefully from its door. What would have happened, I wondered, if I hadn't made my way here in the naïve expectation of a delicious meal? If a home hadn't been needed for Kyi Kyi, or Franc hadn't been taken on as a student by Geshe Wangpo, or Sam hadn't shown up at just the right time?

There was something mysterious and quite delightful about the chain of events that had led to this point.

And the events that were to continue.

Later in the evening, when the initial surge into the bookstore had calmed down, Serena walked over to where Sam stood with a commanding view of the gathering.

"It's been a wonderful evening!" She radiated happiness.

"Hasn't it just?"

Sam, I noticed, managed to avoid the floor and was looking directly at her, a helpless smile on his face.

Then they both started to speak at the same time.

"You go," she said.

"N-n-no." He gestured to her.

"I insist. You first."

From my vantage point, I could see flecks of red dotting Sam's neck. Like storm clouds gathering, the flecks melted together to form a crimson wave that rose steadily toward his chin then suddenly halted.

"I was just going to suggest," he began, louder than strictly necessary. "Seeing as we'll be working together—"

"Yes?" Serena prompted. As she brushed her hair back, her earrings glinted under the lighting.

"It would be a nice idea, but only if you had the time . . . "

"Yes?" She nodded encouragingly.

"I mean, maybe we could get together sometime. Perhaps for a meal?"

She laughed. "I was going to suggest exactly the same thing."

"You were?"

"It'll be fun!"

"Friday night?"

"Deal!" Leaning forward, she softly kissed him on the cheek.

Sam squeezed her arm.

At that moment Franc emerged from the crowd behind them. Meeting Sam's eye over Serena's shoulder, he winked.

Back home that night, I took up my usual position on the windowsill. The Dalai Lama, having returned from Delhi, sat on his chair nearby, reading a book.

The window was open, and along with the fresh scent of pine, there seemed to be something else in the air. A hope of things to come.

Watching His Holiness read, I couldn't help thinking, as I often did in contemplative moments like these, how very fortunate I was to have been rescued by such an amazing man. Images of that day in the streets of New Delhi still arose unbidden. Especially those final moments when I was wrapped in the newspaper and my life force seemed about to leave me.

"Most interesting, my little Snow Lion," the Dalai Lama remarked after a while, as he closed his book and came over to stroke me.

"I am reading about the life of Albert Schweitzer, who was awarded the Nobel Peace Prize in 1952. He was a very compassionate man, very sincere. I have just read something he said: 'Sometimes our light goes out, but is blown again into flame by an encounter with another human being. Each of us owes the deepest thanks to those who have rekindled this inner light.' I agree with that, don't you, HHC?"

Closing my eyes, I purred.

ABOUT THE AUTHOR

David Michie is the bestselling author of *Buddhism for Busy People*, *Hurry Up and Meditate* and *Enlightenment to Go*. All have been published internationally and are being translated into many languages. David was born in Zimbabwe, educated at Rhodes University in South Africa, and lived in London for ten years. He is married and based in Perth, Australia.

www.davidmichie.com